G000300635

OF FIRE

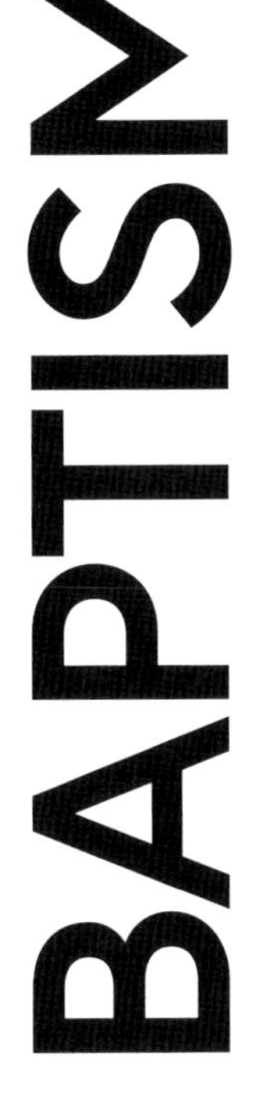

A year living & working with Duran Duran

IAN
LITTLE

edited by
Charles Kennedy
and Steve Thorpe

Cover design by Murray Wellwood

Copper Blue Design www.copperbluedesign.scot

Inside design by Simon De Rudder

ISBN 978-1-9160396-4-3

Astral Horizon Press www.astralhorizon.co.uk

CONTENTS

	Introduction By Hazel O'Connor	5
	Preface	7
1	From Economy To First Class: Time In Sri Lanka With Simon Le Bon	13
2	My First Musical Adventure: Supertramp In LA	23
3	Gallery Studios & Real Beginnings	33
4	Working At Gallery & Learning To Produce	41
5	The Making Of Avalon And Jealous Guy	49
6	How I Started Working With Duran Duran	69
7	Is There Something I Should Know?	75
8	Mixing Is There Something I Should Know?	87
9	Ian Little - The Early Years	95
10	The Perfection Of Being	101
11	Crisis, What Crisis?	113
12	Writing & Recording With Duran Duran: South Of France, Spring 1983	117
13	Main Album Recording At Air Studios: Montserrat, Summer 1983	135
14	Working On Island Time	153
15	Mixing Seven And The Ragged Tiger	165
16	Seven And The Ragged Tiger Side One	175
17	Seven And The Ragged Tiger Side Two	193
18	Production Principals	203
19	My Fall From Grace	207
20	Take My Breath Away Giorgio Moroder, Sparks & LA	215
21	Homeless In New York City & New Beginnings	221
	Acknowledgements	231
	Music Outreach Project: A Brief Synopsis	235
	Duran Duran Discography 1981 To 1985 Compiled By Steve Thorpe	237

Pictorial Press Limited / Alamy

INTRODUCTION
BY HAZEL O'CONNOR

I first met Duran Duran when they were the opening act on my Breaking Glass tour in autumn 1980. My manager had met with their managers, the Berrow Brothers, who also owned a club in Birmingham called the Rum Runner and it was agreed that my tour would be good for them to give them profile.

My band and I really enjoyed going out to the side of the stage to watch them play our favourite, Planet Earth. It was unfortunate for them that my audience was very Punk and they were little bit more New Romantic with frilly shirts a go go, which elicited some hostility from my audience. But as we can see now, what's in it for the shirt? It's all about the songs not the clothes.

Touring with the boys was great fun. They didn't have a big budget and travelled in a campervan. They drew straws every night to see who got the one hotel room they could afford in the budget, and they would all use the room in the morning and have their showers. Simon Le Bon used to stress about losing his voice and asked me questions about what do I do with my voice. I told him to keep drinking the tea and get that frilly shirt off!! They dumped the frills and donned the Antony Pryce suits (nicked from Roxy Music!) and voila, the rest is history.

Within six months of that tour, they had signed a huge record contract and had a hit single in the charts with Planet Earth (I guess I knew how to pick hits, should have been in A&R). I was proud to have been an early champion of what turned out to be one of the biggest bands in history. Hope you enjoy Ian's book, I'm proud to be an early champion for this too. Happy reading!

PREFACE

Firstly, I want to thank you for picking up this book.

I had several reasons for writing it. I want to give you, the people who have been fans of Duran Duran for many years, a view of what went into making the records I helped produce for them. I also want to try and give you an impression of how they came across as people away from the spotlight. Remember, they were only in their early twenties, and just two albums into their careers. They'd had success in the United Kingdom and most of Europe but had yet to make a real impact in the United States. They were well on their way to becoming established in the pop hierarchy but were in a period of transition. Their fans were growing up, the young teens that flocked to them in the beginning having turned into more mature, older teenagers by the time they would be releasing their next album. In addition, many bands have historically stumbled on creating the third album.

The first album contains all the songs that came from the excitement of their formation, the songs that got them signed and expressed their identity. If successful, they are then guaranteed a second album, which will hopefully ride on that same wave of excitement, as Rio clearly did. For their third album, a band must then return to the well of inspiration and become creative all over again; and in Duran Duran's case, they also needed to appeal to a more adult fan base. This meant developing a way to consistently write hit songs and create a formula / identity that they could repeatedly draw upon to have long term success.

I came away from the period I spent with them in 1982-1983 full of fondness and respect. I learned a lot about each of the five Duran Duran members as individuals. What I also realised was that each of them, while naturally having their own character, also understood the importance of the collective to their ongoing success. Once bands have money and taste real success, members can easily forget the power of the collective and instead start to believe they alone are the reason for their success or at least, that they don't need the rest of the band to continue having success.

I could tell they still seemed to be good friends, all focused on the same goal of global domination. They were confident without being arrogant, still fresh enough to enjoy the spoils of success, not yet jaded or overly indulgent. No riders stating live panthers, fresh orchids in January, or M&Ms with all of the brown ones taken out!

I also want to tell the story of how I came to work in the music industry in the first place; became noticed by this band at such an important time; and of the making of two of their most important records – their first number one single Is There Something I Should Know? and their first number one album Seven And The Ragged Tiger.

My other main motivation in creating the book is to raise funds and awareness to help create the Music Outreach Project (MOP). This consists of a portable recording studio (Digital Audio Workstation) that can be set up in any community space and teach young people looking for direction how they could start making music. In addition, it will make them more aware of all the other creative fields they could get into. London is a world capital for the creative arts, such as film and television creation, fashion, illustration, packaging, writing, and more. I have included a full synopsis of my proposal for the MOP elsewhere in the book in English, Italian and Spanish so any of you living in other countries, with the right skills, could start up a similar project in your hometowns. We all know the problems we are facing here in London of disenfranchised young people losing direction and turning to crime or joining gangs, but this is a phenomenon that is sadly not unique to the United Kingdom.

I'm sure a lot of you have children of your own now, and I feel confident, judging by the majority of replies I received when first suggesting the idea of the book and the MOP, that you care about the paucity of opportunities the current generation of school leavers face. A lot of those I'm doing this for have left school without the academic qualifications they need to find meaningful work and are resigned to stacking shelves or flipping burgers, not as a temporary step but without hope of progression. I want to give these people the opportunity to express any creative spirit they may have. In my experience, young people have an artistic spirit that is not encouraged because they've never had anybody to inspire or encourage them directly. It has thus remained a dark art, mysterious, unknowable, unfulfilled.

In addition, it's a sad truth that artistic creativity of any kind is rarely acknowledged at schools, let alone encouraged. With some mentoring and proper guidance, that creative ability has the capacity to lead to opportunities that with hard work can generate the possibility of meaningful, paid work, and perhaps create a new generation that could surprise the whole world, or even save it.

Finally, I must inform you, that if you are a Duran Duran fan that would normally only buy officially endorsed products, this is not an official book and does not have the band's support. Hopefully enough of you still buy it and having just found out that you own an unofficial book, are not freaking out, putting your foot through the TV or wrecking your homes!

Regardless of their decision to withhold their imprimatur, I wish the band nothing but continued health, spiritual wealth and happiness. I've long since made it clear that there is nothing in this book that they should be ashamed to see be made public, and the only person I criticise in these pages is myself.

In many ways the trajectory of my career may have been more manageable if I hadn't been given the chance to help produce them at that time. Hindsight is a wonderful thing and it's easy to say it was too much too soon; I had only been working in the recording industry for a little more than three years. Having said that, you never know if you'll ever have another chance to work with a band reaching the peak of their commercial powers, as Duran Duran were then, so I'd have had to have been very confident in my future prospects to turn such an opportunity down.

So, that's about it for this preface. After reading the whole book I hope you enjoy listening to Is There Something I Should Know? and Seven And The Ragged Tiger having gained a new insight into the way they came into existence. You'll also learn about me; how I found my way to music in the first place; my work with Roxy Music on both Jealous Guy and their seminal Avalon album; and how I was given the chance to work with Duran Duran.

Finally, there's material throughout the book about the path I've been on since my mid-teens which can best be summed up as being the pursuit of Truth. Those of you that have seen any of my posts on social media will know, I am perfectly content, spiritually almost as rich as it's possible to be, and regard life and every new day as a massive blessing. Peace and love to you all. Enjoy!

Beach at Gaulle

1
FROM ECONOMY TO FIRST CLASS
TIME IN SRI LANKA WITH SIMON LE BON

At that stage in my life, in 1982, I'd only ever looked across at people checking in at the First Class counter with envy. This time, I stood in that exclusive short line to check in for a long-haul flight to Sri Lanka, expensive ticket in hand. I had been chosen to produce the next single by Duran Duran, the biggest, hottest band in the world, and I was on my way to meet the singer, Simon Le Bon.

Even back then, the difference in space and service you received flying First Class was enormous, from the extra room thanks to a huge reclining seat, to the levels of service, including meals served on china rather than in a plastic tray - washed down with an unlimited supply of champagne. It makes the whole trip a real exercise in indulgence rather than a cramped ordeal. Even before you board the plane you have access to a luxurious lounge to while away the time until, ahead of other passengers, you board the aircraft.

The flight was amazing and I soaked it all up, hardly wanting to sleep in case I missed an opportunity to try some of the goodies on offer. Once we landed at Colombo's Bandaranaike airport, after being ushered through immigration, much to my amazement, we walked back out onto the tarmac and things became even more incredible.

My travelling partner Michael Berrow, one of the two brothers managing the band, and I were led to a waiting helicopter. I remember thinking, this can't be for us, it must be for someone else. It was for us and we were soon levitating back into the air. After crossing the outskirts of Colombo, our pilot aimed for the coast. He dipped and soared as palm trees bent seaward. He tried to stay as close to the shore as possible, giving us the most exciting ride imaginable, providing us with wonderful views of this lush island's beaches. Along with the pilot's flamboyant style, the turbulence pushed us around a fair bit. It certainly was, for a lover of all things fast like me, an incredibly exhilarating ride.

As if the means of transport were not exciting enough, the reason for the trip was to meet Simon Le Bon, who was taking a holiday there. The band's management had decided that the first thing I needed to do, as the band's new co-producer, was to get to know the lead singer. But rather than wait until Simon was back in London for us to meet and chat, I was flown halfway across the world with no expense spared. Not a bad first day on the job. I later realised that it also gave Simon time to learn more about me, my ideas, and what I could bring to the party, so that he could report back to the rest of the band when they were together again in London.

The helicopter ride was over all too soon as we landed on the beach at Gaulle. We were immediately surrounded by excited children that came splashing into the surf to greet their special new guests. The kids already knew white men meant rupees, but those that arrived by helicopter must be worth big rupees! The heat was scintillating and the smiles and laughter of the children helped complete the sense that I'd escaped the winter gloom of London and landed in paradise.

Michael and I walked up the beach to our majestic hotel, a reminder of the island's colonial past, when Portugal ran the country. My room was all dark wood with shuttered windows. A large, four poster bed covered by a mosquito net stood solidly while a lazy spinning fan circulated refreshingly cool air around the room.

Talk about a dream beginning. Picture the scene. One day I'm cleaning up the mess generated after a twelve hour session in Gallery Studio, owned by Roxy Music's Phil Manzanera; the next, having been flown halfway round the world in First Class and then by helicopter, I'm standing in paradise, my toes squeezing the smooth-as-silk sand, while looking out across the azure blue sea from the edge of a beautiful island off the southern tip of India. Talk about culture shock!

Despite the effects of the flight I only took a short nap, eager to meet Simon as soon as possible. I was introduced to him by the hotel pool. He was relaxed and happy with a beautiful girlfriend at his side, this being prior to his long-term relationship with Yasmin Parvaneh.

We seemed to gel almost immediately. Maybe it was being in this beautiful place thousands of miles away from studios or the performances to come, but he was clearly at ease. I felt the same, and I was delighted to be in Asia, excited to be at the start of what I imagined would be an amazing journey working with the band. I was blissfully happy.

I had been told that Simon was, for a globally-famous rock star, surprisingly shy on first meeting and somewhat cagey, but once you spent time with him, I was assured he would open up, and only then would I be able to learn more about the real Simon Le Bon.

Before that first day, I'd only seen him in the band's sumptuous videos looking like a Hollywood star from the '40s as much as a modern-day pop sensation. The swashbuckling nature of the locations, especially on a stunning yacht for the hit single Rio (and prowling through the tropical jungle in Hungry Like The Wolf) cast him in that role, and he took to it like a natural.

I sat and talked to the young man from Pinner. He struck me as a likeable guy who was relishing having the time of his life. It soon became clear we had plenty in common. We naturally talked about music, having fun, and life in general. I articulated my thoughts

Anjadora / Wikicommons

on meditation and spirituality which seemed to resonate with Simon. He asked me about my past travels and seemed particularly interested in my time in India. He was curious to understand more about the place and its people. I told him about the overwhelming sense of culture shock I had experienced during the bus ride from Delhi airport into the centre of the teeming metropolis, that despite the grinding poverty that pervaded many, there was a sense of joy about this ancient race of people with their multitude of religions. Being in India was like being Dorothy in the Wizard of Oz – a long way from Kansas.

I could tell from the attention Simon paid to my description of my first trip to a distant country and totally alien culture that he could relate to it, presumably due to the amount of travelling to far flung places he'd already experienced in the couple of years of the band's success to date, especially during the filming of the videos for the Rio album in Sri Lanka. There was a fundamental difference to my travel experience, as Duran Duran were constantly inside a bubble full of people waiting to do this or that and go here or there to meet their every whim. Nonetheless, I could tell he'd felt the dislocation that culture shock creates, and, like many truths, is hard to truly impart unless you're talking to someone who has shared the same experience. Our shared travel experiences became a source of humour and helped a great deal in breaking down any initial barriers that existed between us at that early stage.

Our conversation soon moved on to the task at hand. There were many anecdotal stories flying around regarding the difficulties he encountered when recording his vocals on the first Duran Duran album. He couldn't sing in tune. His timing had been weak. He had struggled to express emotion in his performances. If there was truth to any of it, I needed to find out why. I tried to gain an insight into how he approached recording his vocals. I knew that no two singers were the same and that each had their own way of getting that killer take. Unlike live performances where once sung the moment is gone, recordings are forever and so each performance had to be the very best a musician could muster. And this is even more true for vocalists.

Something I discussed with Simon was how he expressed the meaning he wanted his lyrics to convey. I soon learned that he would adopt the role that he felt best suited a line, much as an actor would. This I found encouraging – Bryan Ferry was very much a method singer and loved to live the role the lyrics suggested. I told Simon I thought that was as good a starting point as any, as it enabled him to inhabit the words and give them a degree of plausibility, to help them sound real. I said I was as interested in the sounds that words made in the context of a song as I was regarding any literal meaning they may have, and this seemed to resonate with him. He said he felt some words just sounded better, sat right and that although important, meaning could be secondary, with which I wholeheartedly agreed. We talked about singers like Bob Dylan or Leonard Cohen, even Ferry, none of whom could be said to be particularly gifted technicians but still conveyed a huge amount of presence.

After a few conversations about working in the studio, putting down vocals and building tracks, we reached an understanding of what each of us felt was most important. I concluded by saying that my goal was to try and make recording his vocals as enjoyable as possible; that my primary concern was to create an environment that he felt at ease with and that we'd take it from there. I also said that I didn't care if the killer performance was the first take or at the end of several hours of work, as long as we got there in the end, which I felt confident we would.

Simon was interested in my work with Phil Manzanera, Roxy Music, and the time spent on the creation of Avalon, their most recent album, of which more later. Simon knew the album well and was naturally full of curiosity about the mechanics of making a record as lush and immaculate, and I discussed many of the techniques, tips and tricks Roxy Music and their producer Rhett Davies had used. I was heartened that when discussing the fine line between perfection and being obsessive, we agreed that when editing vocals, cutting words up into individual syllables was on the wrong side of that line!

Simon was also fascinated with what Bryan Ferry was like, and I expressed my opinion that what people saw, his public persona, was about 90% artifice or image, that he inhabited with consummate professionalism to maintain what the public saw and heard. This act was topped off with about 10% of the real person. This was a deliberate tactic because when people describe frontmen as shy, Bryan Ferry was the epitome of such a person. He hid inside the character created by his clothes and makeup which seemed to give him the freedom to perform on stage with such panache, that he could hold an audience in the palm of his hands, the hallmark of all great performers. Charisma or presence - call it what you will, but that 'X' factor distinguishes all great band leaders or singers.

It's a rare gift, often misunderstood and underestimated in its ability to transform a live performance into a compelling and memorable experience.

Since Duran Duran were already in the business of selling out arena shows, this was an art that Simon was privy to as a fellow member of an incredibly small club of performers, so his curiosity about the craft of another member was understandable.

I knew those weeks in Sri Lanka were the calm before the storm, but I was enjoying every minute and not dwelling on the hard work ahead. Being in Gaulle was gorgeous. The strip between the hotel and sea was criss-crossed by dozens of winding, sandy pathways meandering through clumps of vegetation and palm trees. It was a lovely walk to reach the water's edge and once there, you were greeted by a choice of cafes and bars offering fruit cocktails and local snacks. I had a glorious time; the weather was idyllic, the people beautiful and the place itself was as close to the picture of paradise most of us carry in our heads as to make no difference.

It was possible to rent motorised trail bikes near the hotel. On one occasion when Simon was tackling some deceptively tricky sand dunes on such a machine, the front wheel jammed into the sand and the bike fell on top of him. The exhaust pipe on these bikes is mounted midway up one side of the machine and unluckily that was the side the hot pipe was on, and it burnt into his thigh. Ouch! That incident restricted his movement for a while.

A favourite haunt was a restaurant established by an Australian, designed for the wealthier Western visitors. It was full of genuine, local antique furniture and served up Western-style food (at a price) that was something of a treat compared to the admittedly rather basic (but far cheaper!) local fare. As a strange aside, when we all went to Sydney to finish recording and then start the mixing of Seven And The Ragged Tiger, the owner of that restaurant contacted me at the hotel I was staying at. It turned out that shortly after we'd left, the Tamil Tigers had stepped up their fight against the incumbent government and as part of their tactics had trumped up gun running charges against the poor guy, deported him, and forced him to leave behind everything he'd built up. He lost the lot, forcing him back to his native land a broken man.

All too soon we were on our way back to London. It had been a fantastic adventure and an unexpected beginning to life as Duran Duran's new co-producer. I had met and spent several weeks with Simon and certainly felt I had a good appreciation of his strengths and weaknesses from a work perspective.

Once back in London it wasn't long before we were scheduled to start work and time was booked at Tony Visconti's Good Earth Studio in London's Soho district. But first, I still had to meet the rest of the band.

I was invited to go and see them play the Hammersmith Odeon (now Apollo). I had an Access All Areas (AAA) pass and as the fans gradually filled the auditorium, I wandered around taking in the place, going up and checking the guys mixing the front of house sound, and introduced myself. The excitement built as the place filled up with adoring fans, who'd come to see their idols. I decided the mixing desk was where I'd watch the gig from and quickly made my way there.

Comparisons to the Beatles at the height of Beatlemania were unavoidable. The king is dead, long live the king! Once the gig was under way, any time I tried to go out into the crowd just to check the sound from the middle or back of the hall, I was mobbed. The fans knew that if I'd come from behind the barriers, I must be closely connected with the band. I was totally overwhelmed at being hassled this way just because I was now associated with the guys on stage! I soon gave up on going beyond the safety of the mixing area and the security personnel manning the barriers protecting it, and I watched the gig from there.

At the centre of the unfolding spectacle, the band I saw that night in Hammersmith were a well-oiled, slick operation. It was obvious they had the looks, moves, style and charisma - along with the musical ability and songs - to conquer the world. Simon was already well on the way to becoming the consummate frontman he is to this day.

After the gig, back in the dressing room, as they all bounced in, I could almost taste the adrenalin that such an intense performance generates. This was my first opportunity to meet the other members of Duran Duran. I was genuinely excited to be introduced to the guys individually. They were fantastic, friendly and happy to talk to me, asking how I felt the gig had gone and seemed genuinely as excited as I was about the prospect of working together in the weeks ahead. I expressed admiration for their performance and said I couldn't wait to start working with them. Beyond that I didn't stay long – there were many other people backstage they needed to talk to ("shake and fake" in showbiz parlance) so I soon made my way out, elated by having finally met the whole of the band.

Supertramp covers

© Shutterstock Images

2

MY FIRST MUSICAL ADVENTURE
SUPERTRAMP IN LA

Before I start writing about working with Duran Duran, I want to tell you how I had my first experience of the music business. After travelling in Asia and ending up in Australia, I arrived back in England with my girlfriend of the time. To cut a painful story short, some three months later after a week away from our Chelsea flat (spent building a theatre set for a one-man play) I returned home to discover that instead of hugs and kisses, I was faced with a short note from the love of my life. It said she had gone to live with my best friend and that I had two weeks to vacate the flat, which was owned by her father.

I must admit I was devastated, and it took me several months (in some ways, years) to fully come to terms with the sense of betrayal that came from losing my girlfriend, best friend and accommodation all in little more than a week. Yet, I had to move on. I had to do something.

Here is where the connections I'd made by going to university to study art came to my rescue. I had become good friends with a couple of architectural students, Paul and Allan, and ended up renting a room in Paul and his wife's home. I also started working at the firm the pair had established a few months earlier.

It was practically unheard of for two guys fresh out of college to set up their own architectural practice, normally working for several years at an established practice first, after which, if the wind was in the east, all the planets aligned, and you knew enough of the right sort of people, then maybe, just maybe, you could go it alone!

These two old university friends chose a more direct approach. Paul and his wife both came from wealthy and well-connected families, and between them found plenty of potential clients. They started out not doing new builds, but refurbishments of large mansion flats (a peculiarly olde London form of apartment building), and the makeovers they were doing weren't just a lick of paint and a new three-piece suite. It meant structural changes, the type requiring architectural work to be carried out. I wasn't a qualified architect, but they needed someone who could do a quick watercolour, showing how a variety of layouts and colour ways might look. I had a job.

One of the partners of this fledgling practice knew the guy responsible for the lighting design for Supertramp, a successful British band who had relocated to Los Angeles to further their American career. Supertramp had enjoyed a string of reasonably successful albums, but everyone in their organisation knew that Breakfast In America, their soon-to-be-released new album, was going to power them into the stratosphere. Their label A&M Records predicted a global smash hit, so they had put together a huge world tour that would see the band travel the globe over about eighteen months, playing on just about every continent.

Their lighting guy told us they had put out a tender for companies to submit design proposals for the stage set and lighting rig they would use during this epic venture. Gus, the lighting engineer, suggested to Paul that we submit ideas for consideration. Despite having no experience of such work, we took on the challenge, and went against other firms well established in the field.

Much to our amazement, having never done anything like this before, our concept was chosen. That was the zeitgeist, the times we lived in, new, fresh ideas from unexpected places were the way to go. Excitedly, and somewhat in disbelief, we started to work out the intricacies and mechanics of our design and soon realised what an undertaking it was.

We'd created an incredibly complex design which looked stunning, and now, just a couple of months before the tour was scheduled to commence, we had to deal with one final hurdle. We had to demonstrate that our design could be assembled and packed away again by the team of riggers that would travel with the band. This meant that every element of the stage and lighting rig had to be broken down into pieces no heavier than two guys could manoeuvre with ease. This was a nerve-racking process for us, as our design looked awesome but was far from simple. We weren't engineers and had no experience in the field. Additional pressure came from knowing that several recognised firms, many of which had expected their designs to be accepted, were still poised to step into the breach if we wavered in the slightest.

Having had our design accepted, and on obtaining the contract, we now had to supply a full-sized version of what had previously only existed as a 1/100 scale model. A stage set and lighting rig that could function in the real world was a big challenge.

We were under quite a bit of pressure to demonstrate that our great looking set could function in the heat of battle, on the road. One of the hardest elements of creating a design for such a massive tour was the variety of venues it would be used in. In some cases, it would need to be built as a stand-alone structure in the middle of a football stadium, with the lighting rig on supporting legs, whereas smaller indoor venues provided hanging points that could support the weight of the lighting rig with ease.

Working through the solutions was challenging but helping to solve all the issues we faced in turning our design into a working piece taught me a great deal about problem-solving, and taking any creative endeavour from concept to real world functionality. I didn't know it at the time, but a few years later, dropped into the world of making music, the skills I'd learned working through the problems presented by our design for Supertramp's stage show meant I already understood how to analyse a complex process, and identify the way each component fitted with the next to create a smooth workflow. Those lessons would prove their worth again and again.

As D-Day approached, it became clear that someone from the architects needed to fly to Los Angeles to oversee the trial runs of building and packing away the stage set and lighting rig. The two partners were too busy at the London office, and so it fell upon me to make the trip to the band's Los Angeles base. Well - someone had to do it!

Despite having briefly been to Los Angeles when I was still at university, upon landing at LAX I was slightly thrown off balance by the sensation of thinking you've walked into the draft of a fan heater as you reach the aircraft's door and the balmy heat first hits you, an experience familiar to anyone who's flown to a country hotter than their own.

As I walked out of the airport, I was instantly also struck by the light in LA. To say it was sunny was not just inadequate, it was almost an insult. The sun illuminated everything like a spotlight in an otherwise dark theatre. I took dozens of photos using a manual film camera and when I returned home, I was devastated to discover that my limited photography skills meant that not one shot gave any sense of the sun's intensity and the way it reflected from every surface. Ironic, because it is partly the quality of the light on film that kickstarted the birth of the American movie industry there!

In fact, the light's intensity combined with the neon signs and oversized store logos heightened my sense of being a long way from home. This was alien, not just different. Even though it wasn't my first time in Los Angeles, I still had to keep pinching myself – I really was in LA, city of stars and broken dreams. This time I was there for a reason and not just passing through on a shoestring budget. The oversized Hollywood sign high in the hills above looked down on the action at street level, the hustle and bustle of Sunset Strip, aka the Strip, with its iconic buildings and pavement embedded with metal stars and famous hand imprints, buzzing with energy.

Although I was there on business, I still had limited funds and needed to find a cheap way of travelling onwards to my destination. En route, I had one of the stranger meetings of my life, and my first experience of being totally starstruck. I was going to be staying with Supertramp's saxophone player, John Helliwell, who lived in Topanga Canyon, about twenty miles north of the city proper, up the Pacific Coast Highway towards Malibu. I couldn't afford a cab, so I thought I'd look for a bus to make the trip. I soon learned Los Angeles is not the most public transport friendly city. I was walking along Fountain Avenue, a wide suburban street in West Hollywood parallel to the busy and infamous Sunset Strip, feeling totally lost with no idea how to get to Topanga.

As I walked along the street, I saw two guys standing on the steps of a small church. I approached them to ask where I might find a bus stop. Halfway through voicing my question, I was thunderstruck by the unmistakable familiarity of one of them. "Excuse me, do you know where... you're Bob Dylan!" Just standing there like this was any old day, which of course it was – for him. "Sure, take it easy man," came Dylan's husky reply. Only in LA!

My new friend made it very clear that I needed a new plan if I was to reach Topanga Canyon and find John's house. Dylan went into the church, made a few phone calls, and came back to tell me everything was sorted, that John was driving in to meet me and all I had to do was walk towards the ocean. He gave me a location, in the typical method used Stateside of designating a corner of the intersections of two streets like, in New York, Fifth and Forty-Sixth, in other words the junction of Fifth Avenue and Forty-sixth Street, what could be simpler. Little did I know it then, but that first encounter with a real rock star was to become a common experience for me over the following thirty-five years.

John Helliwell was a great guy. He was still humble despite Supertramp already being huge, especially in the USA, where he'd bought this home. It was a single storey building with loads of glass, perched right on top of one of the Canyon's peaks. The road leading up to the house was more suited to a mountain goat than either his Ducati motorbike or modest car. This meant the building sat on wooden pillars and (for a kid from London) looked far from secure, but was the norm in that admittedly precarious and beautiful landscape where every plot of land was exploited, as real estate was hugely expensive. Topanga Canyon was one of the most desirable places to live.

The views were spectacular. One of my clearest memories is of sitting in the outdoor hot tub in the evenings. Looking inland I could see two or three Buckminster Fuller-inspired geodesic domes (fascinating structures, check them out) that people had made into spectacular homes. Looking westward, you could see the Pacific Ocean. Quite a spot! John and his wife made me feel completely at

Inside a geodesic dome

home. One day we went shopping in Venice Beach and he generously bought me a vintage 1950s-style jacket.

This, my second trip to the States, couldn't have been more different to the first. Once I'd achieved my first logistical goal of meeting up with John, I was treated like a king and enjoyed all the luxury of being associated with a massive rock band. It was very special and generated some memories that are laser etched into my consciousness, not unlike my first memories of India.

I followed John into a massive sound stage and was blown away at the enormity of the operation in front of me. I took particular interest in his role during rehearsals. He was a seasoned pro and as such able to take everything in his stride. The time I spent talking with him only heightened my fascination about the music industry.

The tests of our stage and lighting design all went well. I was all set to fly back to London. Then, out of the blue, John suggested it would be useful (and hugely enjoyable for me) were I to travel with the band for the first six shows at the start of their mammoth tour. I made a quick call to Paul in London and told him that Supertramp had asked if I could attend the first few gigs, just to make sure everything worked as it should. "Good idea Ian, great work, we'll see you in a couple of weeks," came the reply. I was set for my first experience of live music at the highest and biggest level, and what an eye-opener it proved to be.

It was at the tour's opening gig, in Fresno, California that I was given my first AAA pass, and I proceeded to enjoy the freedom of being able to witness this huge concert from wherever I wanted. Supertramp's fans, although just as passionate as Duran Duran's, were not screaming or trying to crawl over the barriers. It meant I could go anywhere, in the audience, beside or behind the stage, at the front of house mixing desk, literally anywhere in the venue, and I took childlike pleasure in flashing my pass, using it as often as possible.

I'm sure you have been to many concerts. You buy your ticket and it either gives you access to a specific area, like at a festival, or to a designated seat in the venue. I'm sure you can relate to how I felt having the freedom to go where I liked for the first time. Although I would enjoy having such unlimited access many times later in my musical career, that first time was something I'll never forget. Being able to pass through any barrier has always excited me.

Going to the dressing rooms to see the band after they've left the stage always gives you a true sense of the energy and passion that a great performance demands. I could sense the adrenalin still coursing through their bodies at the end of such a strenuous performance.

By the time I returned to the UK, a seed had been planted that would, over the next year or so, grow into a solid goal of wanting to work in the music industry in some capacity. I had some ideas that may have led to my working my way up through the recording industry, from small demo studios, acting as a gopher (go for this, go for that etc) had fate not intervened.

I went back to working in my normal role for the architects, creating visualisations of proposed refurbishments, arrangements and colour schemes for grand apartments, but I would often find myself remembering the time I spent with Supertramp. The sense of pride I felt seeing our stage set and lighting rig in action stayed with me, and set me wondering how I could find a route into some form of work that would bring back the excitement I had felt, being so close to music as it was performed and created.

I wouldn't have to wait long. Although I was motivated to find a way into music, I was still suffering from my breakup. As a result, it was only by sticking to my practice of meditating and identifying with the perfection of the moment that enabled me to remain creative and do my work. It also gave me a positive foundation to make goals for the future without ever losing touch with the perfection of the here and now. (Details of this concept can be found later in the book for those seeking more information.)

I thought about sound engineers that work on live shows, both mixing the front of house sound that the audience hears, their counterparts that mixed the sound on stage for the performers, and recording engineers recording the show for possible later release as a live album. I used to sit daydreaming about the Supertramp gigs I'd attended, and of standing by the mixing board in Fresno, California – a long way from my work in London, both geographically and experientially. I had no idea how all that complex equipment worked or even how you learned to use it. It all seemed out of my reach.

From my water colour renditions of ritzy interior schemes for the architects, the road into the world of music was far from obvious. However, I was becoming more and more determined to achieve my goal and various possibilities were fermenting in the back of my mind and growing day by day.

Aerial view of St. Anne's Court/Gallery Studio

3
GALLERY STUDIOS & REAL BEGINNINGS

One fateful weekend Paul attended a society wedding and bumped into an old school chum, Phil Targett-Adams, better known to Roxy Music fans as Phil Manzanera. Paul and Phil had both attended a private school in London, so were old friends, but hadn't really kept in touch, especially as Phil was now a huge pop star. If you don't remember that era, it must be hard to appreciate just how big and influential Roxy Music were, inspiring bands like Duran Duran, not only musically, but their glam rock clothing and imagery being an obvious influence on the New Romantic movement that followed.

Phil explained to Paul that he'd bought St. Anne's Court in Chertsey, Surrey, a fantastic 1930s Art Deco house that contained, in its 14-acre estate, an 18th century coach house that he was having transformed into a recording studio. He was concerned because the architect he'd appointed seemed out of his depth. The building was heritage listed, meaning the exterior appearance had to be preserved. The trouble was that the building had no roof and was at that moment surrounded by scaffolding. According to Phil, it had been that way for almost six months. This was costing him a fortune and it seemed even from his layman's perspective that little progress was being made. He asked Paul if he'd come down and cast his eye over the state of affairs at the site.

Paul asked me to accompany him on the visit to Phil's estate. As soon as we arrived it was obvious that things were not right. No work was being carried out. Even the scaffolding itself was in a poor state of repair. The shell of the building looked precarious, and with no roof, the interior was a total mess. There was no sign of the intended layout, or much of a work schedule.

Paul looked at me, shook his head and instantly declared that we needed to take charge of this, or his old friend was going to be massively out of pocket. After a thorough survey of the site, we went and found Phil. Paul gave him the bad news. Change was needed. That much was clear, but the Royal Institute of British Architects has strict protocols about replacing one architect with another midway through any given project. We'd have to make a case against the incumbent practice and lobby RIBA for the right to take over the contract.

In the end, with work at a standstill, this proved relatively easy. RIBA had no problem deciding in favour of our request for a change of architect as everything we had reported was in accordance with their strict rules and regulations. We were awarded the contract and all previous plans were transferred to us.

Once we'd taken control of the project, we started from scratch with a blank sheet of paper. The existing plans we eventually received from the previous (and now somewhat disgruntled) architect showed a real lack of imagination. The use of space was woeful, although one of the key features of the building was that at one end of the proposed live room were two huge windows. It's a rare treat for musicians to have natural light during a session in a studio, so our design retained this feature. The fact that the coach house was on Phil's own land avoided any concerns about levels of ambient sound leaking out into the surrounding area.

The two architects, with some input from me, did a fantastic job of creating a unique studio that utilised the space in an efficient and creative way. Once it was finished and I stood in the control room, my already firm interest in the music industry was reignited and it was at this point that serendipity, plain old good fortune stepped in. Phil was the guitarist in Roxy Music and Roxy Music were 'My Band'.

I loved everything they had done, had all their albums including the members' solo albums to date. I knew every track, every note, inside out and upside down. I asked Paul if he could inquire if Phil had some time to talk to me about working in the music business and he agreed.

I sat down with Phil, somewhat star-struck, and began to tell him about what I heard in his and Roxy's albums. I talked about key sounds, elements I thought worked well, and asked him question after question about how various sounds and effects were achieved. To his very great credit, Phil listened patiently and answered every one of my enquiries.

After literally three hours of this, he stopped me and said something like, "You are listening to music and hearing the individual component parts that make up the whole sound. Most listeners don't hear music at that level of detail. You certainly have a chance of making a career for yourself working in studios."

I was amazed and felt vindicated that all my dreams hadn't just been pure fantasy. All I needed now was to find an opening in a suitable demo studio, start making tea for the guys that worked there, and learn what I could.

But then Phil came up with an alternative option. The studio was new, full of equipment worth about £500,000 and fitted with an alarm system that was state of the art for its time. The only problem was that part of the protective shield the alarm gave the studio was based on movement detection. This was great in theory. Anybody breaking in would trigger the system as soon as they took a single step. In practice however, being on top of a hill, the location was often subject to strong winds which could trigger a false alarm. When the alarm went off it automatically dialled up a mechanical phone link to contact the local police station.

This would happen at night when the studio was empty, so Phil had to summon his dogs and run as fast as he could from his house to the studio and cancel the system before the phone had finished dialling the police. It was a race against time that wasn't much fun. Various attempts at de-sensitising the motion detectors just rendered the system impotent, with all the insurance implications that created. So, the problem of an over-sensitive alarm system remained.

Phil was about to embark on a three-month tour with Roxy Music, during which his wife would be alone in the house. The design for the studio included an office, shower room and kitchen. So, incredibly, he asked if I wanted to live in the studio while he was away so the alarm wasn't needed, and his wife could sleep in peace. Then, if by the time he returned, I had managed to understand how the studio worked, we could talk again about the possibility of my working there as an assistant, a sandwich maker, and tea provider. Included would be the possibility of me being able to use the studio myself if Phil or a client wasn't doing so.

This was my opportunity and as opportunities go, they don't come much better. Forget working my way up through demo studios. I was starting at a state-of-the-art 24-track facility, designed and built to the highest standards. The work that was created there would be final master recordings by signed and established acts, destined for commercial release. It's hard to convey just what a difference it made to my prospects to be starting work in such a place, rather than, as was usual, some kind of new band demo facility. This was the equivalent of being fast-tracked to the final of X Factor or like playing Monopoly, being stuck on the starter squares only to pick up the Pass Go card and zipping around the whole board in a single leap. I'd not just been dealt a straight flush; I had been given keys to the whole casino. Naturally I turned him down...no, no, of course I accepted with a gleeful smile and couldn't stop thanking him until he walked off back to his house.

Once Phil left on tour, I was faced with the baffling prospect of trying to figure out how to produce a sound out of this complex system. The desk would have been more at home on the Starship Enterprise. The speakers could take your head off. The whole thing was a complete mystery to me. I didn't even know how to switch it on.

I soon came up with a cunning plan. All the equipment must have been made by companies with technical support staff that would know all there was to know about their operation. I'd call them. The problem was I needed a pretext. The equipment was brand new and had been set up and tested when first installed. There was nothing wrong with it.

So, I had to be cheeky. I phoned the company that manufactured the main desk and told them it wasn't making a sound, without letting on that the only reason was because I didn't have a clue how to make it do so. I stressed that this was Roxy Music's studio, so they better sort things out quickly!

They sent a guy out who turned up with a van full of testing gear and introduced himself. What seemed to be the problem? Well, I didn't know, I was new and wasn't sure if I'd hit the right buttons or not. He looked at the desk, looked at me, pressed one button (the power switch) and the test tape that was spinning filled the room with perfect sounding music. He looked at me with a raised eyebrow and was soon on his way.

I used this technique until I could make everything work on my own and manage not to alienate any of the equipment suppliers. In fact, I think they were quite happy to be dropping into Roxy Music's studio, and I became friends with a few of them. I was off and running.

Phil had left me several old 2" tapes that worked on the 24-track and told me I could use them to record various sounds while I figured out how things worked. There were a few guitars, some synths, and an early Roland drum machine. I was not a musician (nor am I to this day), so I couldn't actually play anything well. My inspiration came from one of the original members of Roxy Music who'd gone his own way after their third album, Brian Eno. Like me, Brian had studied the visual arts, and I remember reading an interview with him where, when asked what instruments he played, he had replied, "The studio."

That simple idea became my inspiration. I adopted his approach, and used the ability to record on each of the 24 tracks separately to build up a complex melange of sounds that no one could ever actually play. I started putting tracks together, none of which could be called music in the conventional sense, but which fascinated me and had parallels with some of the weird stuff I listened to and was heavily into.

There was one piece I was especially pleased with but felt lacked a focal point. Every track I made was instrumental, I can't sing to save my life so didn't even bother with that as a possibility. What I did have were various cassettes of people talking including one by a guy who called himself Bubba Freejohn, a self-proclaimed guru. The cassette contained a talk he gave about death and how it was not the negation of life but its natural consequence. It was wonderfully weird, and I proceeded to record short phrases onto a 1/2" tape which I'd then spin into the multitrack. The sampler, a piece of equipment that would make this kind of thing a standard technique, was still years away, so I had to spend hours trying to make each phrase sit right in the track as close to being in time as possible.

Bubba Freejohn's talk was called The Central Proposition so I named my track with the same title. After an all-night mixing session, I went straight up to London without sleeping and to the offices of a small independent label called Beggars Banquet.

As a result of enormous success with Gary Numan in 1979-1980 in particular, Beggars Banquet had just started a couple of other imprints including Situation Two, brand new and run by a guy called Peter Kent. I played him my track and to my amazement he said, "Yes that's cool, I'll release it." I was stunned. My first recording was destined for commercial release. "So, what are you calling yourself?" This wasn't something I'd even considered and hadn't a clue.

My first idea was Possibly An Arab. The reason for this was because I am adopted and had black hair (greying now alas!) and a dark, swarthy complexion. I didn't look British really. If anyone asked what my nationality was I often quipped, "I dunno, possibly an Arab?"

Peter said, "It's a bit of a mouthful. Think of something shorter."

Through the first-floor window behind Peter's shoulder, I could see an Indian restaurant across the street called New Asia. "New Asia," I barked. "I'm called New Asia!"

"That's better," agreed Peter. "More snappy." And so New Asia was formed. I signed a contract on the spot. As he had enough budget available for a 7" picture sleeve, Peter sent me to a graphic designer named Alan McDonald, who came up with a bright orange design with a squiggle, a small black and white picture of a Chinese Coca Cola advert, and a hyphen for my band name.

The single Central Proposition came out in 1981 (catalogue number SIT 2) and Peter sent me to New York for a week to do a series of interviews on college radio. I stayed with a friend of his and had cabs available every day to take me to the respective colleges. It was my first trip to New York and I had the time of my life. The radio hosts were often a bit mystified by my music but were still enthusiastic and, with the endearing optimism that makes Americans so likeable, always gave me a big build up. You can hear it now, "Just flown in from London England, we now have the mastermind behind New Asia..."

The single didn't sell terribly well, but the whole experience was both eye-opening and exhilarating. Those same DJs also started playing the B-Side (Here + There Now + Then) which was basically a drum machine, a bunch of feedback sounds, delays and other effects without the vocals.

The Roxy Music tour ended. Phil often came to the studio without his keys and as usual rang the buzzer for me to let him in. I ran to the door, opened it and stuck out my hand with a copy of my single, resplendent with a picture sleeve. I was bursting with pride, like a kid showing his dad an outstanding school report card. "What's this?" he asked.

"It's my first single!"

"You mean to tell me you've not just learned how the studio works but have made a record, secured a deal, and had it released?"

I had passed the test Phil had set for me, pole-vaulted over it in fact, and I could start work as his studio assistant. My incredible apprenticeship had begun.

Leesmithies / Wikicommons

4
WORKING AT GALLERY & LEARNING TO PRODUCE

I started working and living at Gallery in 1979 and immediately my whole life changed. After creating the first New Asia single in 1981, I then negotiated a deal with Situation Two and Phil to produce an album. The label offered me a budget of £5,000 which Phil agreed to split with me and gave me use of the studio whenever it was free. I started work on recording immediately, and over the coming months put together a collection of tracks.

By this time, I had worked with several musicians and bands that were either recording demos or working on their own projects. The great thing about starting at a studio of that level was that music being created there tended to be of high quality, often destined for major commercial release, or at the very least part of a writing process to create songs that would be released later. It meant the people that started to turn up were established, successful and immensely talented. I learned so much very quickly from the likes of Rhett Davies, Roxy Music's producer, and naturally Phil himself, who would come over most days and want to write or mess around, trying out ideas and writing new material.

Although I had created the single on my own, and had already started work on several new pieces, I decided to invite some of the superb musicians that had come through Gallery to take part in recording on my album. The credits looking back on the recording are impressive: Pete Glenister on bass (Kirsty MacColl); Chester Kamen on guitar (session great); Charlie Morgan on drums (Kate Bush); and Phil Manzanera himself on guitar. I really wanted some tracks to have vocals, and so I asked a guy called Ben Watkins and a girl called Ouida to sing a track each.

The results were mixed. Ben was pretty good, but sadly despite her best attempts Ouida didn't have great pitch and the track she sang on, although full of energy, is not hugely tuneful. The result was a very odd mixture of half normal songs and more of my own electronic meanderings. The full track listing was: Waiting For Surprise, Chant For Running, The Time Has Come, Wheel Of Life, Mystery Passing Through, and Angels Dream Of Eternity. Side Two started with the title track Gates, followed by Balance, Dancing On Empty Clouds, Triamazikamno, No Hiding, Lost Heart, and Discovered Soul.

The album Gates was released as a vinyl LP in 1982 (catalogue number SITU 3). It wasn't a hit, although to be fair it was never meant to be. It did receive some decent reviews in the more indie-orientated fanzines of which there were many, and Lynden Barber wrote a full page article in Melody Maker (July 10th 1982) where he described the album as an "...imaginative combination of loose improvisation, spikily twisting themes, sound collage and drum machines...underpinned by the tension of modern industrialism," as well as going into detail about the creative processes I used as a non-musician. Because many of the tracks were based on simple drum machine patterns, DJs started to play them late at night in clubs, not only in the UK but in far off cities including Chicago, Detroit and New York. Regardless of the almost total lack of sales, the experience was priceless. I also loved the cover which was created by the same designer who did the single. I'm somewhat proud to have recently seen copies of the single on sale for over £10, including a white label test pressing on Discogs for £20 – not too bad!

Gallery was not quite like a normal commercial studio. Phil did not need to generate income from the facility; for one thing it was on his own land so he had no additional rent to pay. A large part of the construction and equipment costs had been funded by Phil and Roxy

Music's management company E.G. to create a place to record Flesh + Blood, Avalon and any future albums (albeit the latter never came to pass, with Avalon being their swansong).

Consequently, it was mostly used by Phil's friends, musicians he already knew, or who were introduced to him by other associates he trusted. During the three years I was there, some would bring their own engineer, while others would rely on my limited but creative approach.

Among the more memorable people to turn up were Kevin Godley and Lol Creme, formerly half of the band 10cc, famous for the hits Rubber Bullets and I'm Not In Love among many others, the latter of which used multiple layers of vocals to create a totally unique sound and a prima facie example of using the studio as an instrument. They were both incredibly talented individuals in multiple disciplines, true examples of polymaths. They would have a connection to Duran Duran in the years that followed of course, directing the video for Girls On Film, the uncut version of which was so steamy that they had to tone things down before MTV agreed to play it (naked girls with ice cubes and mud wrestling was apparently a bit too hot to handle).

When they came to Gallery, it was on the back of the recent single Under Your Thumb which had peaked at number three in the UK charts in October 1981. As recording artists, they were an absolute riot, constantly stoned and always playing jokes on me and each other. It was a lot of fun, and despite all their fooling around, they still managed to come up with some decent material.

One game Lol came up with was when trying to play a stab on a keyboard that occurred at the end of every bar. He would hit the keys then set off at full tilt to try and run around the entire room and arrive back in time to hit the keys again at the end of the next bar. Seeing him scrambling around, grabbing onto the ends of the desk to swing himself around the corners is an image I'll never forget. I'm not sure to this day if any of what they recorded with me was ever used but they certainly left an impression. I saw yet another way of approaching the craft of songwriting.

The other time I was as starstruck as I had been bumping into Bob Dylan while lost in Los Angeles was unexpectedly having dinner with Paul and Linda McCartney. This mind-blowing episode was even more shocking for me as I was still very new to working with successful and famous people. Phil Manzanera had poor eyesight and didn't enjoy driving at night, especially on the country roads around his home in Surrey. As a result, whenever his wife Sharon and he went to London for an engagement they would ask me to drive, drop them off, amuse myself for a few hours and then collect them for the trip home.

On this occasion, much to my surprise, Phil told me to dress up and look my best. It wasn't Christmas or my birthday so I had no idea why he wanted me to be suited and booted. I put on my only suit, a beautiful electric blue silk number that Phil himself had given me, and with some trepidation drove the car round to the house. Nothing was said other than Phil telling me to head for The Caprice, a popular haunt, one of London's more exclusive restaurants at the time and a place I had taken them to many times before. Once in the area, instead of heading for the main entrance of this swanky joint, Phil told me to look for somewhere to park, as close to our destination as possible. Phil was instantly recognised by the maître d' who gave us a warm welcome and led us to a table in a secluded spot towards the rear of the place. To my amazement, the table we were joining already had two occupants. I was speechless - those two people were none other than Paul and Linda McCartney.

I knew the McCartneys were old friends of the Manzaneras but never in a million years did I expect to be in such exalted company. I'd already worked with Bryan Ferry, and met plenty of famous people, but Macca? This was a different league and I was totally star-struck! I don't think I could even talk for most of the meal and had to keep pinching myself to remember I was really there and awake. Quite an experience. Whatever term you use to describe star quality, the X factor, charisma, it matters little, when you're in the presence of someone that has it, you just know. McCartney was indeed pop royalty; The Beatles changed the face of popular music in a way no other band has ever done. As to why Phil invited me along, I've often wondered about that. Perhaps it was his way of saying I belonged in that world (not that I was in any way shape or form as talented as the great man) and that I was moving in the right direction to have a career, and the potential to be as good as I wanted to be. Or maybe it was just him and Sharon having a laugh, throwing the new boy in at the deep end. Watching me struggling to keep my cutlery under control created much mirth whenever they recounted the tale!

I was present at Gallery for the creation of a very successful album called Wired For Sound released in August 1981 by Cliff Richard. The songs had been written by Alan Tarney who also did all the arrangements and produced the whole affair. As an example of the different ways that stars can treat you, whereas by a sequence of events and a lot of generosity by Bryan Ferry - on the sleeve of Avalon I received a Production Assistant credit; Cliff decided in all his wisdom to credit me as Assistant Engineer, Sandwich Maker and Table Tennis Coach! It sounds quite light-hearted and was I am sure intended without any malice, but I was trying to build a career and a reputation and it felt a little demeaning. As a person Cliff was not my favourite individual, he unfortunately appeared somewhat insensitive to other people's feelings from my point of view at the time.

On the other hand, Alan Tarney was one of the nicest and most determined people I ever had the pleasure of working with. At some point he booked Gallery for six months to write new songs. He would arrive at about 10am, walk around either strumming an acoustic guitar or vamping at a keyboard until he had, by about noon, the basis of a song.

Although initially Alan had chosen the bass as his main instrument, he was not only a great singer but a consummate multi-instrumentalist. He would record lead vocals plus quick multi-part harmonies in the choruses once he had the words, then "la-di-da" the verses. The chorus is the hook, he told me, and needed from the beginning of the process if only to ensure the underlying chord progressions had real potential, before writing the rest of the song.

I was impressed with his whole approach to writing. He was disciplined, treating the process very much as a job of work. He was determined to come up with a new song every day. After a month, working Monday to Friday, as far as my naive ears were concerned, he'd come up with twenty potential hits. When I told him this, he rebuffed my comments and told me that of the twenty written, only two were keepers, and challenged me to pick them out. I had recordings of all the songs and I listened hard to each of them. After my deliberations and at the end of my allotted time he asked me to come to a decision. I told him which two of the twenty songs I considered usable, and to my delight, he said I was finally starting to recognise what it is that makes the difference between a good or adequate song and a potential hit. Our working relationship blossomed, and Alan seemed to respect my judgement more. He started to ask for my opinion on each new song he penned.

Alan taught me so much about writing songs, regardless of genre. He started with structure, saying that if you could find a structure that worked, you could hang any ideas you had on it. He used the analogy of building a house, and how scaffolding was in place to create a structure to support it during construction. Regardless if you were adding guitar phrases or synth lines, it was so much easier if you were using a solid framework to give your song a structure you already knew worked. Your structure gave you the ability to be able to assess the part's relative worth quite quickly. Certainly, more quickly than if you just jammed away looking for inspiration and then if a gem came up, not knowing what to do with it!

Alan's way of working, very methodical and disciplined, wouldn't suit everyone, but it sure worked for him. He wrote many big selling hits over his career, including Wired For Sound, My Pretty One, Some People, and the number one single We Don't Talk Anymore for Cliff Richard. Alan also produced hit singles for Barbara Dickson, Leo Sayer, Squeeze, The Dream Academy, and Matthew Sweet, as well as many of a-ha's global smashes – Take On Me, The Sun Always Shines On TV, Hunting High And Low, Manhattan Skyline, I've Been Losing You, Stay On These Roads, Cry Wolf, Train Of Thought – one of the most impressive run of hits in the history of pop music.

Throughout my career, I've used a secret Alan shared with me. He said that every overdub, and every new part added, should lift the intensity of the track by a quantifiable amount. If it doesn't, it's just filler and needs to be removed. The number of times I've had to apply that rule, often to the chagrin of the musician who'd created it, are too many to count. But in every case, when it came to mixing the track, the value of not having the part there always proved to be the right decision. There's only so much space in a track at any given point. Each part needs room to breathe.

Many of the artists who Alan produced or wrote songs for worked in what is known as the middle of the road (the genre shorthand is MOR) and had a huge audience. To see someone create songs designed to appeal to a mainstream audience was an education in itself. My own interest as a music fan tended towards the artier end of the spectrum, so this was an early lesson that to be a good producer, you need to put your own taste to one side and judge any form of music on its own merits. Make the music work for the audience it is aimed at.

One final word on Alan's attitude to life (and the origins of my dubious credit on Cliff's album). When Alan first arrived, I was the table tennis king. Bryan Ferry could give me a decent game but no one else came close. Alan started playing me every day, and very soon I realised he was watching my every shot and learning them. By the time he left after six months, he was beating me on a regular basis. His last lesson for me? Even in a casual game of table tennis, he demonstrated the same drive and determination he applied to making music. It's the attitude you need to succeed in life.

I'd spent three years living and breathing music creation and literally sleeping in a recording studio. I had been lucky enough to have worked with some incredibly talented people, I learned from some of the best engineers, producers, musicians and writers around at the time. Along the way I was lucky enough to be intimately involved in the production of what is still considered a timeless, classic album – the wonderful Avalon by Roxy Music.

Roxy Music

5
THE MAKING OF AVALON AND JEALOUS GUY

Without doubt the high point of my time at Gallery Studio was my involvement in the creation of the Roxy Music album Avalon in 1981 and 1982. Considering the building tension between the three core members it's hardly surprising with hindsight that it turned out to be the last Roxy Music album. My first work with them, still very much as the tea boy, was when the band recorded the song Jealous Guy earlier in the year as a genuinely heartfelt tribute to John Lennon, after he was murdered in December 1980 at the entrance to the Dakota Building, NYC, where he and Yoko Ono lived.

At this point in their career only three of Roxy Music's founding members were left in the band - Bryan Ferry, Phil Manzanera and Andy Mackay. Vocalist, guitarist and saxophonist respectively. These three guys from the original line up had appeared on every Roxy Music album released since the band's ground-breaking, eponymous debut, way back in 1973. Seeing them on Top Of The Pops playing their debut single Virginia Plain was a revelation, made me an instant fan and had a huge influence on my life and pop music in general. It looked and sounded like an art installation had invaded the BBC. I was 18, home from university, and not only did I love it, what made it even more exciting was that my parents didn't get it at all. The look and sound of the band was aptly described in the music as a mixture of rock and roll and science fiction. Despite being regarded as part of the glam rock movement, I always felt they were far more experimental than the movement's mainstays like T Rex, Slade, Sweet and even Bowie during his Ziggy period. Roxy Music were more out there; their albums, with songs from their first release like Ladytron and The Bob (Medley), were closer to Surrealist soundscapes than pop music. To my mind they were unique.

In later years Phil and Andy's presence had been more down to legal reasons than because of any working relationship existing between the three members. To be able to use the Roxy Music name, Bryan Ferry had to have the participation of the other two, and if only for commercial reasons he knew the benefit of the Roxy Music name as opposed to another solo affair, as the band's product consistently outsold Ferry's own. It was still a good match musically, as Phil and Andy helped retain some edge and a taste from their formative years that Bryan, left to his own devices, would often lose. Fully unleashed, he tended to inhabit his lounge lizard persona a little too much, producing music more at home in a cocktail lounge than a rock concert. The disparity between sales was no coincidence and testimony to the lasting influence the pair had on Bryan's song writing and production, helping retain his original vision for Roxy Music and their loyal fan base.

But by 1981, after recording and touring the Manifesto and Flesh + Blood albums, they'd had enough of each other and were barely on speaking terms. It's not that there was any real deep-rooted animosity between them, more that Phil and Andy, who were still very close friends, realised they no longer had anything in common with Bryan or the lifestyle he sought to live, socialising with Britain's blue-blooded aristocracy. From the beginning everyone understood the situation for what it was, Bryan knew of his obligations to include Phil and Andy, and they in turn knew they were indispensable if another Roxy Music album was to ever see the light of day.

The loss of John Lennon brought the three remaining members together in the studio earlier than planned when they decided to record their cover of Jealous Guy. They had started playing the song live after his tragic death and it soon became a fan favourite. It was recorded and released at the start of 1981 and was a far simpler, less produced record than the album that followed it. It was also my first taste of working with the band I had been into for almost a decade. Along with Bryan, Phil and Andy, Gary Tibbs came in to play bass (later to become a member of Adam & the Ants for Stand And Deliver and the Prince Charming album).

I thought Andy Newmark played drums on Jealous Guy but I can find no credits to confirm that now. It may well be that a Linn drum machine was used and I am confusing one of the takes he performed on Avalon (where he played on all but two tracks) for him playing on Jealous Guy.

My abiding memory of the sessions will always be the recording of Ferry's vocal and his whistling over the outro. I, like all in the control room for that session, was in tears. The palpable sense of loss, the realisation that Lennon had been taken away from us for good, was still hard to assimilate. Our shared sense of loss was intense, Lennon's legacy would live on but all the clichés were true, it was wrong, unfair, way too soon for him to be taken away. Witnessing Ferry express his sense of loss through his moving performance will always go hand in hand with my memories of learning of John's sudden death. And unlike on most of Bryan's vocals, I don't remember a great amount of time being spent on editing the performance either. It remains one of the most emotional and intense sessions I've ever had the privilege of being part of.

I was still very much just the tea boy at that stage. I could sit in on all the sessions unless other duties took me away. Unlike many assistants, every free minute I had was spent in the control room, absorbing as much as I could from the immensely talented people around me, all with so much to teach me and little or no time to do so! I worked hard to make sure everyone could sense my enthusiasm and passion, which made it easier for someone to try and teach me something. I was genuinely grateful and by attempting to put into practice tips revealed, tried to make it clear they weren't casting pearls before swine. I took in as much as possible while still taking care of my more mundane duties.

Roxy Music had split up, seemingly for good after the release of their fifth album Siren in 1976 just as punk rock was born. However, they had reformed in 1978 and recorded two albums, Manifesto and Flesh + Blood, promoting both with substantial tours. The next time they reconvened was 1981 to record Jealous Guy, which went on to be their first and only UK number one hit single, ensuring the band had a wider appeal than ever before.

Behind the scenes, cracks were starting to show. Hardly a harmonious starting point for an album, but they were disciplined enough to work together when required - seeing collaborating very much as a job of work, admittedly a not unpleasant one. Being involved in a creative undertaking was what they loved, even lived for. There was no doubt that Bryan was the main driving force, his was the vision that had brought the three of them together for what turned out to be their last hurrah, but Phil and Andy went above and beyond with their contributions to the finished product.

From the start it soon became clear that some ice breaking was going to be necessary. The first manifestation of this came when they each booked their own separate slots at Gallery to work on writing and recording songs to be put in the hat to be considered for inclusion on the album. So rather than, as with most bands, getting together and playing around to see what transpired, instead the three would each spend time alone with me, writing and recording ideas and working them up into finished songs.

Which songs would find their way onto the album would primarily be Ferry's decision to make later, once everyone's best efforts had been submitted. One of Bryan's stipulations was that he would only ever sing his own lyrics, if not in whole then certainly in large part. This meant two things. Firstly, every song on Avalon is completely or partly written by Ferry. Secondly, that credit split meant he earned far more publishing royalties than either of the other two, one of the reasons the three never recorded together again (although any resentment this may have caused never materialised during working hours). In addition, record sales were high enough in the 1980s to generate a much bigger revenue stream than today, and this was divided more equitably than the song writing income between the three members. Plus a reasonably large global tour from which they would also earn from ticket and merchandise sales, again made the split more democratic.

For me this arrangement meant I was the only person to be present during all three songwriting sessions. Rhett Davies, the band's producer was very much Bryan's man and was only in the studio when working on Ferry's demos, and not for Phil or Andy's. Instead I was given the responsibility to engineer for them. I saw this as a massive show of confidence by Rhett when it became clear that he had no concerns about my ability to do the job. This was to be the first of many opportunities I would be afforded during the making of Avalon. What an album and pool of talent to learn the ropes from.

As I remember it, the first into Gallery to put down his demos was Phil, natural enough considering he lived less than 100 meters from the studio! Each of the three had their own way of coming up with new songs. For Phil, being a guitarist, he looked for inspiration or a starting point in an interesting chord progression or picked riff, a melodic phrase that he could then build a structure around and come up with the heart of a song. He was a real joy to work with, always open to suggestions - whether it be me messing around putting delays and other effects onto his parts, often totally destroying his guitar sound; or presenting him with a carefully programmed drum machine pattern, to give him a groove to play to, either might act as the spark to inspire his natural creativity. Aware of the need to provide Bryan with the basis for a hooky chorus, Phil would always put a lot of effort into structuring his songs, making the dynamics strong and compelling. His South American roots sometimes gave his songs a mildly Latin feel. To my still musically naive ears I felt he'd come up with several strong contenders. The final choice would be made later once Bryan decided if any of Phil or Andy's songs spoke to him, suggesting lyrics, especially for the choruses.

The track of Phil's that eventually made the cut became one of the singles lifted from the album, Take A Chance On Me. A superb addition with its long, haunting intro full of Phil's somewhat menacing guitars, some reversed and joined by Andy's great clarinet phrases, sparse drums, tom fills and underlying drum machine pattern that all build to a drop, that introduces the picked guitar phrase that runs through the verses. There are several layers, often consisting of no more than sound bites that create wonderful detail and interplay. Different parts weave around each other, working together to form a sense of intrigue and mystery but never sounding cluttered - and therein lies the secret to the album's success and durability. Like much of Avalon, the intro has a cinematic, widescreen feel to it, which gives way to a relatively sparse first verse leaving Ferry's vocals plenty of room to draw you in. I'm not going to dissect every track but have tried to use this song as a guide to what makes the album so rich, luxuriant, full of depth and detail. To say it was a labour a love doesn't really come close.

Even on probably the album's most lightweight and commercial track, the opening More Than This, Phil adds some guitar chords and phrases that go some way to provide a bit of edge and weight it would otherwise lack. This was typical of the way Phil and Andy helped reign in Ferry's tendency to go more saccharine in trying to appeal to a wider audience, much to the dismay of Roxy Music's hardcore fan base. The same can be heard throughout the album, there's always a healthy tension created by the way Phil was usually pushing at the edges of Bryan's comfort zone with raw sounds and a more aggressive approach.

I had the pleasure of spending many hours working with Phil on his own material. The high point came when he asked me to engineer and in effect co-produce his solo album, Primitive Guitars, in which he explored musical themes inspired by his South American roots. That and the fact I was there to hear him lay down his parts meant that I recognised his input, distinct from other guitar parts played by Neil Hubbard and the contributions Bryan added. Even without such inside knowledge I think most music lovers will recognise the various styles of each guitarist and start to spot the parts each of the three added to the overall sound, at least after a few hearings.

Andy Mackay had been Roxy Music's saxophonist from the beginning, giving them what was at the time a slightly unusual sound;

although by no means unique, there weren't too many bands that had a sax or wind player as a permanent member. Plenty used brass sections as a feature on a particular song and would take a section on the road if budget permitted, but having Andy as a key member gave Roxy Music a sound of their own. His classical training showed in his approach to songwriting. As a non-musician, I was initially quite intimidated by his ability to write scores for his or other people's parts.

He made a huge impression on me, starting with an intimidating matter-of-fact attitude on first contact. He drove a Bristol car, which for any petrol head is a very expensive, ungainly but superbly hand-built English limousine. Typical of the man, it was an unusual choice, few would make the kind of investment required to own a Bristol as opposed to a new Mercedes or some other, more easily recognised status symbol. As I was totally into cars, I used my appreciation of his choice as an ice breaker and soon gained his trust.

In truth I needn't have worried, beneath his slightly austere front he was relaxed and easy-going company. During our time together he couldn't have been nicer or more accommodating when working with me, even if I occasionally lost the plot or struggled to keep up with his flow of ideas. Of the original band, Andy was the most versatile, making a very decent living for himself working on projects like television themes and soundtracks. Amongst his more notable successes was a TV series that he composed the music for and produced called Rock Follies, and its sequel Rock Follies '77, a show about an all-girl rock band searching for success.

Working on songs to be considered for Avalon, Andy used his full spectrum of musicality to try out different ideas. Looking back on the time he spent writing with me at Gallery, it's impossible to think of him as being just a saxophone player, and I certainly don't mean any disrespect to that happy breed by saying it. It's just that normally they are seen as having relatively minimal parts to play and their influence on the music is similarly limited. That was never the case with Andy, and it was a pleasure and education to hear the way he used quite traditional methods to create interesting, inventive songs. Thinking back to the early Roxy Music albums, it's impossible to imagine those records without his unique input.

In the end, from Mackay's demos, Ferry decided to use the song While My Heart Is Still Beating, and the instrumental closer Tara. The former begins with some sparse sax lines, a programmed Linn drum machine joined by percussion, piano and abstract reversed guitars as it gradually builds through the verse to the low-keyed chorus. After this, the bass asserts itself before the second verse begins and the track opens up. During the verse you can hear Neil Hubbard adding beautifully subdued guitar picks, typical of his input on many of Avalon's songs. They work wonderfully with Phil's reversed phrases, giving the track its haunting, surreal sound. I had to check that it is in fact 3:51 in length as it sounds much shorter. Often if a song sounds shorter than it is, it's a good sign and shows that it is almost perfectly structured. You're left wanting more. The spaciousness of the track does not sound empty but instead represents a beautifully crafted lack of parts. Science tells us that what we call empty space is far from being nothingness but is full of the stuff that makes stars and planets. So, the spaces throughout Avalon are far from simply empty. This may sound like pretentious twaddle and probably is, but what I'm trying to draw your attention to is the way the gaps in between parts have a sound, beautifully crafted by Bob Clearmountain's mixes. But more of that later.

Andy's sax line in the pre-chorus gives the song a strong theme. A common thread throughout the album is on display here. Ferry's lyrics are at times hard to decipher, but that takes nothing away from the impact of his singing, or perhaps vocalising better describes his sound here; meaning is secondary, instead his performance oozes atmosphere, a constant throughout the album and one of his enduring skills. Not all his lyrics are so hidden, but clarity never gets in the way of expression with Bryan.

Although Phil is credited with writing just one (and Andy two) of the ten songs that make up Avalon I think, they both played on the whole album and had a major influence on the final product. Their contributions are essential to it being a Roxy Music album and certainly not just for the legal reasons. Their personalities, tastes and musical values, and the passion with which they applied themselves, did in the end create a kind of chemistry by proxy; a reactive force that bent and warped Ferry's vision away from being too smooth or indulgent, giving the album enough edge, enough cut and thrust.

When it came to Bryan's writing, Rhett Davies engineered and I was his assistant. Once Rhett arrived, my heart sank somewhat. Naturally I was excited to finally have Ferry in the studio but whereas I was able to run my own show when I was in with Andy or Phil, this meant that my duties were downgraded to making everyone comfortable with mugs of tea and coffee, going goodie shopping, and perhaps rolling Bryan's joints, a skill for which I definitely had a certain panache that he quickly recognised and employed to good effect.

As things transpired, I needn't have worried about playing second fiddle. As time progressed, Ferry became more and more interested and confident in the value of my ideas and feedback whenever I could find the courage to express them. When I did speak, what I said was for the most part well received. This meant I was soon spending more time in the control room, as others were being sent to the shops or asked to make subsequent brews.

The first time this shift in Bryan's assessment of my value to the project happened came one day when I found him in what had originally been intended as an office for the studio and had been repurposed as my room. He was flicking through my immaculately kept vinyl collection which included all new releases that had caught my attention during the time I'd been at Gallery. He could tell that I had my finger on the pulse of post punk music from the late 70s and early 80s. I was eight years younger than Ferry, and never one to miss a trick, he saw that he could use my knowledge of contemporary bands to catch a feel of the zeitgeist. He started by asking me about certain albums and how I rated various artists. Eventually I cut to the chase and offered to make him a cassette of what I felt were the best tracks from a selection of releases covering the previous year or so. The success of the first tape meant these mix tapes became something of a tradition that I would produce for him when asked. The frequency of his requests related to how long he spent driving. If he stayed at his Fulham mews house a tape might last a few days, if he drove to his country house it might only last one day. I was happy to oblige and gained great pleasure in introducing him to new acts I was into, that I felt he'd appreciate. The discussions we had after he'd absorbed each tape are some of my most cherished memories. Sharing a spliff discussing PiL or Depeche Mode with one of my teenage heroes = surreal. How blessed was I?

As the principal writer for Avalon, Ferry was on a mission to produce what I think he knew at the time would probably be the last Roxy Music album. As such, in his quest for perfection that all artists will recognise, he was acutely aware of not letting any little nugget of inspiration escape. During the time I was involved in his song writing, the process was divided into two methods. The first, and more conventional, involved him turning up at the studio with close to fully formed songs that he'd give Rhett, and asking him to listen to them and provide as much feedback as possible. Ferry was still not quite as relaxed with me, so what happened was Rhett gave the tape to me in secret with the same instructions Bryan had given him.

I mention this because it says a lot about how Bryan, basically a shy person, dealt with fame and how he saw his public persona. Despite us having already shared several personal, open conversations listening to records in my room, he still wasn't comfortable giving me a cassette of his demos. Rhett knew better, that if he stopped and thought about it, to give me a copy made perfect sense. There were times, undoubtedly low, often chemically induced points, when he would start talking about himself in the third person, as if he were some royal personage never to be addressed directly. Fame can have a very strange effect on people and all those so afflicted in the spotlight develop their own coping techniques to deal with the pressures of having even the tiniest part of your personal life and relationships being scrutinised through the lens of the tabloid press.

The songs he presented to Rhett (and me) had been written while he was in some idyllic spot in Ireland with his soon-to-be wife Lucy. The story goes that the concept of Avalon, the connection with the Arthurian legends and even the cover, were all conceived during that time in Ireland. In order to maintain the Roxy Music tradition of always having a woman or women on their album covers, Avalon has a photo of Lucy wearing that wonderful Viking-like helmet. It is quite a picture and must have taken some real effort for Lucy to hold her head still!

The other way Ferry came up with songs was very different. It started out when Bryan, Rhett or even me, came up with what we dubbed a moody synth, either on its own, or more often accompanied by a programmed drum pattern, something that I had been doing long enough by then to be pretty good at. A moody synth sound was crafted from a blend of a pad sound, based on an organ, string or voice synth preset, combined with various effects such as echo in time with the drum machine, or a chorus or other modulation effect in sync with the beat. Adding delays to the drum machine also helped oil the groove, creating an even more absorbing sound.

I learned so much from Rhett during this time about the judicial use of effects to emphasise some aspect of the original sound it was applied to and designed to create a more distinct and characterful tone. I often find myself discovering analogies in the visual arts, and so in this instance you can talk in terms of hue and light, texture and the tactile aspect of paint applied to canvas. Sound can be described in such detail, ultimately it's what you can hear and the feeling it gives you. An album like Avalon had so much love poured into it, each and every sound is a work of art in its own right. When starting out with all these goodies to hand, the tendency is to overuse them to the point where they drown out the sound being treated and wash all over other sounds as well, taking up way too much space. This results in the mix losing definition, you're just hearing all the outboard gear chattering away and the source is lost. I learned to hear how more subtle use of such treatments worked. This was a big part of the learning curve I went through during the creation of Avalon.

Resonant, with plenty of movement, a successful moody synth would make a simple chord progression come to life. It's hard to say what it was that made such a sound work but boy, did you know it once it was humming! Bryan would start swaying and letting out vocal accompaniments that would at once get the creative juices flowing. Many times I can recall the hairs on my arm would tingle or I would uncontrollably shiver.

There's no question that it was very easy for us to just become lost in the sound of a groove and a single, well-crafted pad sound as Bryan messed around playing various chords, adding counterpoints and harmonies. In fact, it was probably the fact that Rhett smoked far less than Bryan and I that saved us a lot of time, however much Bryan and I may have been enjoying it!

I was in heaven to be working with one of my musical heroes, and having a teacher in Rhett who could see my passion and desire to learn and consequently was always giving me pointers, helping me learn good practice, production principles and as many engineering tips as I could absorb. It doesn't get much better. Little did I know it then, but to think that because of those sessions, Bryan would end up insisting I was credited as Production Assistant rather than tea boy or general dogsbody. It still brings tears to my eyes all these years later. I don't really know what to say.

The challenge was to try and structure this wonderful atmospheric soup into a song and this was where the hard work began. The way it was accomplished was both time consuming and came close at times to being boring, but was redeemed because of the end result; and every spark of inspiration, however simple it may have first appeared, was captured for consideration.

Rhett and I recorded sections, each one maybe twenty seconds long, of Bryan playing these moody synths, from the two-inch master onto a cassette. I kept a written log of each section, and by doing so, made sure any characterful or moving progression that showed potential was preserved and notated. By combining various progressions that seemed like they might fit together, kernels of songs were born. We continued over a period of weeks with a lot of listening and experimenting with endless combinations of different snippets. Songs started to take shape, appearing out of the mist and stumbling into each other as if by magic.

As each tune reached a certain point, where it had a solid framework, a beginning, middle and end, it would be given a working title and was then considered ready for development by the addition of layers of parts and sounds, along with the all-important lyrics from which hooks would be formed. As soon as possible, Bryan would record a guide vocal even if the precise melody or lyrics were still to be finalised. This had the effect of fixing a song's structure like mortar setting a brick wall.

With popular music, especially of the type aimed at a more mature audience as Avalon was, singles were first and foremost marketing tools designed to sell the album. They didn't need to be standalone monsters that sold millions, although that was fantastic, it wasn't a necessity. It was album sales that well-established bands, late into their careers as Roxy Music were in 1982, looked for.

The next section I'm going to describe was to me the most organic, sumptuous and eye-opening experience of recording music I've ever witnessed before or since. You only need read the credits on Avalon and consider the wealth of musical talent that was cajoled, encouraged and sometimes seduced into bringing that album into existence, to appreciate the finesse with which Ferry realised his vision, curated parts and produced one of the last century's most sublime thirty eight minutes of popular music ever committed to tape. Rhett played a massive role and as was confirmed by Bryan's credit for me I made a difference as well; alongside all the superb musicians that performed on the album, and of course Bob Clearmountain who mixed it. I'm not going to go through each track on its own but rather try and put across what was unique about how Ferry and Davies approached producing.

During the latter stages of the album's gestation, I learned how to not just listen but hear the most subtle nuances of sound and performance. Parts are created to work alongside each other in such a way as to allow each to be heard without ever sounding too exposed. Everything sits perfectly in its own space, placed there by subtle use of frequency adjustment and careful use of a myriad of effects, to create the sense of space that a given sound exists in. All these minute adjustments are made to position each sound, created in the first instance to fulfil a certain role musically or rhythmically, then placed in its appropriate place where it can affect the whole track as intended.

One of the musicians I remember working with most clearly was bassist Alan Spenner, whose performances are even more remarkable because of the circumstances in which they took place. He would often not turn up on time and it would reach the point when it was decided the cavalry needed to be sent out to find the man. With any normal session player that would result in them being replaced, but Alan was different. He was late because he was hung over, often still drunk, but his unique ability meant all was forgiven. I would first drive to his flat near Maida Vale, wake him up and get him to the studio. Once delivered, and often with me crouched behind him in case his balance deserted him, he would then play drop-dead gorgeous bass lines, bang on time and full of invention. An almost Jekyll and Hyde transformation took place. He delivered and played on seven tracks including the big ones. Despite or perhaps because of his state, his playing was superb - on the beat, full of movement and when appropriate, as in The Space Between as funky as fuck. Please do not think for a minute I condone excess alcohol abuse or that it's in any way a prerequisite to great performances (Alan himself sadly died aged 43 of a heart attack); but as a player he was unique, and his ability to inhabit his instrument while so far removed from a normal functioning state is one of life's abiding mysteries!

I can't mention Alan without thinking of drummer Andy Newmark, at the time one of the world's most in-demand session drummers, who played on all tracks except To Turn You On, which was Rick Marotta, another superstar session drummer, and closing track Tara which uses a drum machine. Newmark remains one of my favourite drummers if only for his less-is-more approach. He could hold your attention with a simple kick and snare and hi-hat to create movement and dynamics. When it was appropriate, he could play patterns as complex as anyone but I've never heard anyone capable of maintaining a groove with such a minimum of effort. It was almost like legerdemain, watching him you'd think he was barely touching the snare; the speakers told a different story, as out came an ear-bending thwack! He was a breath-taking, magical and memorable delight to hear in action. Andy is a true legend, and probably still best known for being a member of Sly & The Family Stone in the 1970s; his playing is also beautifully demonstrated on Beauty Stab, the underrated and timeless second album by ABC released in 1983.

Another contributor worthy of mention was Fonzi Thornton, one of the best backing singers ever, Aretha Franklin's longest serving sideman who also sang on records and tours by Michael Jackson, David Bowie, Diana Ross, Steely Dan, Change, Robert Palmer and Chic among countless other legends. He performed with such panache and style, complementing Ferry's vocals perfectly, being just emotive enough without crossing the line. You never felt he was competing for the spotlight, just nailing stunning performances on demand. A real pro. Again, what a privilege to have witnessed him perform. The tone of his voice and the subtlety and precision of control he employed was like strawberries and cream.

The only time I wasn't involved was when Roxy Music went to Compass Point in Nassau, Bahamas. There they added parts from several additional, wonderful musicians whose contributions I had to wait to hear! Eagle-eyed owners of Avalon will notice that no credit is given to any recording having taken place at Gallery Studio; only Compass Point and The Power Station (where Clearmountain mixed the album) are on the sleeve. As I didn't go to Compass Point, but am credited as a Production Assistant, this bears witness to the work done at Gallery. I have my own theory for this omission, but as I have no proof it will have to remain one of life's little secrets!

Allowing a song to grow, from a simple metronomic click, a drum machine, a riff, a chord progression, a guide vocal; all the way to a finished, mixed, track ready to release, is a difficult trick to pull off. It's up there with any creative process, like a painter starting with a blank white canvas and creating an image that has a life of its own with the ability to touch you emotionally; or turning an architect's scale model into a building you can ride an elevator to the 100th floor in.

If you don't understand the steps you go through, or know the process involved, it remains a mystery. In this book I've made several attempts to demystify that process but really, it's like telling you how to ride a bike. You just get on and eventually ride it! It's impossible to convey the feeling of finding your balance, but once you've cracked it, you finally simply know how to ride a bike.

The time and attention to detail spent recording and curating the parts and performances that went into Avalon verged on the insane or obsessive. As an example, consider one of my favourite contributors, Neil Hubbard, a guitarist brought in to complement Manzanera's work. He had the ability to play the simplest of ad libs, tiny flicks of a string, the odd picked line that would be used to fill a gap between vocal lines or create an accent at a key point. He would be asked to play through each track five or six times depending on what he came up with on each run through. Once the consensus was that there was enough material recorded to work with, Bryan, Rhett and I were let loose on the parts he'd left us. Like kids in a sweet shop, we would dive in and start running through each take he laid down, looking for that gem, be it a killer lick that fizzed across the track like a lightning bolt, or a cry sounding like the call of a whale thousands of miles away guiding you into the song.

In fact, if you listen carefully there are many instances of Phil and Neil combining their styles to create a sound greater than the sum of its parts. One example is The Space Between. When the vocal eventually comes in there's an amazing blend of two guitar parts, one playing a little picked line out of which emerges a Nile Rodgers & Chic-style rhythm part that hooks into the bass to create sumptuous waves of groovability. And so it went on, each musician equally gifted with their weapon of choice, brought in by Bryan or Rhett because of what they were capable of, and all of them delivered. Most were already familiar with each other from working together on previous recordings, or on the road.

Once each song felt complete enough, the time came for Bryan to nail his lead vocals, along with double tracking, harmonies and ad libs. The remarkable thing about Bryan's approach to his own performance was that he was even more stringent than when assessing the performances of others. It is no exaggeration to say that I have heard Bryan use different syllables from separate takes to compile a single word for his lead vocal. Often, even Rhett would look across at me and shrug his shoulders, but we'd always do as asked and not once do I ever remember Bryan getting it wrong. Such subtle nuances made the world of difference, sometimes even when variations were so subtle I often found myself, still new to this level of detailed assessment, unable to fully appreciate the differences until the final result was created and sat so perfectly in the track.

Bryan was searching for a sound he had envisioned from the very start and knew it the minute he heard it. When I listen to Avalon now, knowing the time spent on making his vocals sound as they do, I'm reminded of his pursuit of a dream where no compromises were tolerated. Expression and emphasis spot on, overall effect compelling.

After the band moved on to Compass Point, I continued with my regular life at Gallery until the time came for the final stage. Mixing was taken on by the legendary Bob Clearmountain, working at the Power Station studio in New York, a facility that must rank alongside Electric Lady as being amongst New York's finest and most storied. As well as mixing, I seem to remember some tracks had drums recorded there as well. This may be one of music's urban myths or perfectly true: that Clearmountain had a full kit bolted to the floor in the live room, completely mic'd up and ready to go, so that with no more than some tuning by the drummer (a skill that all experienced studio drummers are well versed in) he was ready to roll the tape knowing that he could produce a sound ready to mix.

The final stage in any album's gestation, the mix, is when the final reckoning takes place; when all recorded parts are scrutinised one final time and then the great juggling act is attempted. Trying to balance each part against the others, first in volume and frequency, then in more subtle terms of tone and hue, as in a painting. It was a Herculean task but one that Clearmountain was a Ninja level master at achieving. My memories of the mixing of Avalon are like lightning in a thunderstorm. The whole experience became far clearer for me when

I listened to the album back home, and particular sounds, effects and the overall sound of the album really hit me in the cold light of day. It was almost as if the sessions themselves were too much to take in on their own, and I had to be transported back to the magic by listening to the whole of the album itself.

One of the most charming stories of the album's creation was in New York when Bob Clearmountain was well into final mixing. Like so many such encounters, it was pure chance. A voice was heard emanating from another studio in the Power Station that can best be described by the lyrics of the classic Tavares single, Heaven Must Be Missing An Angel. The sound was otherworldly, ethereal, in fact just like an angel, soaring into the heavens, with a sound so pure and soulful you couldn't help being moved.

Her name was Yanick Etienne and she was a Haitian singer, in to record some traditional music. She spoke no English but with the help of a translator she was let loose on the title track. The rest is timeless history, magic and sublime, her parts adding another dimension that takes the coda of the song into the stratosphere. What a find.

Top bands used Bob Clearmountain as their mixing engineer because he was the best. He seemed to be oblivious to genre or style, instead taking each sound like a diamond in the rough that he would then cut and polish to create the gems that you hear on any records he touched. The guy was a magician. To balance the elements that comprise a track was hard. To do it with panache, creating a feeling and atmosphere, all the while maintaining the highest technical standards requires the genius of someone able to hear and understand the detail and foundation of every sound, almost at a molecular level. Bob Clearmountain was that guy. I had the sense that his touch was so light that he caressed the mixing board, when moving a fader or turning a knob you sensed he was aware of trying not to bruise the object of his attention. He heard the very slightest changes his actions made as he painstakingly built the mix, treating every part as if it could make or destroy the whole.

There are a huge number of tools at a mixing engineer's disposal which is both a blessing and a curse. Used knowingly equipment such as compressors, limiters and other tools that control the dynamics of a sound can help create definition and identity. Used sloppily, with guesswork and a lack of skill, they can make it impossible to find a balance. I can't go into the way each step of a mix is approached or I'd be writing a book on that subject alone. Instead I want to return briefly to the spaces, the emptiness in the mix, because to me this is the most difficult thing to achieve. Assuming the mixer knows how to get a great drum sound, can make the bass pump, and sit the vocal in the right place on top of the music, the breathing space is what will make or break the finished mix. Get it right and you have Avalon. Get it wrong and you have an album that may sound superficially acceptable but in reality is cluttered or will become tiring, and quickly sound dated, the effects being of a time and place. Some, like the drum sound on Bowie's Let's Dance for example, stand the test of time; others I won't name, do not!

The high point of my time working on Avalon came when I was asked to do an extended mix of The Main Thing for the 12" single. I was stunned and shocked but thrilled! My first attempt was to say the least a nervous and somewhat underwhelming effort and I was told, gently, "It's too normal, we want to hear you on this." Phil had played the New Asia album to Bryan and Rhett so they wanted some of my weirdest best! I never really found the courage to go all the way. Even though the version that was released is a bit more experimental than my first attempt, it's still too tame. However, the fact it was released at all is one of my proudest achievements. Maybe I should ask if I could have another go? I'd kill it now!

Avalon was my rite of passage and they don't get much better than an all-time classic album. I still lacked experience, something that only time and hours of work can help you to gain, but the principles of good song writing, of listening at a level of detail I had never dreamed possible, to hear musicians so far beyond the run of the mill - all of this helped transform me from a studio boy, sweeping up at the end of a session, into someone for whom anything was now possible.

Bob Clearmountain

6
HOW I STARTED WORKING WITH DURAN DURAN

After I had been working at Gallery Studios for three years, a beaming Phil Manzanera walked into the studio and called me aside. He announced with a straight face that over the next few days, I would receive a call from the managers of a band called Duran Duran. I honestly thought he was joking. The biggest band in the UK was going to call me? "No chance!" was my reaction. But my view changed when Phil told me the story that lay behind it.

As was well known, Roxy Music were an obvious influence on Duran Duran. Both bands were touring Europe, and by chance were performing in the same city in Germany on the same night. Phil had met a couple of the members of Duran Duran – I understand it was Nick Rhodes and John Taylor – in a nightclub.

They began to tell Phil about where they were at on their journey with the recording of their third album, after recording two albums (Duran Duran and Rio) both produced beautifully by Colin Thurston. They felt they knew enough about the processes involved and had amassed enough studio experience so that now, they were ready to take more responsibility to produce their next record, and were looking for a new co-producer, someone with fresh and creative ideas.

Phil had seen my contribution to the creation of Avalon, to his own projects, and the work I'd done with the paying clients that had come through the doors at Gallery. On considering the body of work I'd done to date, despite still being relatively new to the recording industry, he had no hesitation in suggesting they should check me out. Bless him, if it hadn't been for that chance meeting and Phil seeing something in my approach to production and making music, I wouldn't be telling this story at all. I owe him an awful lot.

A couple of days after Phil's astonishing pronouncement, one of the Berrow brothers who managed Duran Duran did indeed call me, and after a brief introduction, said that they would like me to remix a track they had recorded. They had booked time at Good Earth in Soho, the studio owned by producer Tony Visconti who made his name producing T-Rex, and most notably David Bowie's 1970s output, which changed the axis upon which the world turns. Adam Ant recorded a superb album Vive Le Rock there a couple of years later in 1985 which Tony Visconti also produced, but sadly it wasn't a commercial success.

I'd only ever worked at Gallery, so I was immediately nervous about the prospect of doing a mix somewhere else. After the phone call, I sought out Phil for his advice on how to approach the task. He told me there would be an engineer there who would be able to show me how everything worked, and that most studios are more or less based on the same foundations. Another excellent tip was to take some music I knew well with me and play a few tracks through their system to establish an idea of how it sounded. I could then set some mental benchmarks for the sound of the system and the room, especially at either end of the spectrum – bass guitar and synth down the bottom, hi-hats and tambourine at the top. I could also get my bearings by listening to tones in certain frequencies – 1Khz will tell you a lot about how midrange instruments and vocals should sound. Then to just go for it!

Thus briefed, I turned up at Good Earth at the appointed time and walked into the control room. The empty Ampex box for the 2" multi-track tape of the Duran Duran track was sitting on the sofa, the tape already loaded onto the 24-track machine. I'm not entirely certain what the track was after all these years; however my educated guess with hindsight is that it was a then-unreleased instrumental called Faith In This Colour (which ended up as the B-Side to Is There Something I Should Know?).

I introduced myself to the assistant engineer and sat down to wait for the band to turn up. After about 45 minutes, with the allocated studio time passing, I asked the assistant if he knew when the band was coming. He replied that he didn't think they were. What?! Or more precisely WTF?! In the three or so years I had spent at Gallery, I had never been asked to do a mix for a band where at least one of them wasn't present to give me feedback and discuss their vision for the track, and what they wanted me to try and achieve. Did they like that snare sound, were the drums too loud, how about the guitars, was there enough reverb on the vocal, did they like the effect I was using? To me that kind of feedback was what gave me an idea for the direction I was taking the mix, and whether it was as they'd envisaged.

How was I supposed to do a mix that Duran Duran would like, if they weren't there to pass comment as the process took place? I decided to take a breather and walked up the stairs out into the street. I walked around for a few minutes, smoked a couple of cigarettes - trying to compose myself and decide what to do next.

I returned to the studio, still frustrated and somewhat angry. My main thought was that it was totally unfair to expect me to create a mix they would like if they weren't going to be there to comment and share their views on my progress. So, I made the decision that if they couldn't be bothered to turn up, then the outcome couldn't matter much to them, so I was just going to do as I pleased. As I was more into indie, punk and new wave than pop, I set out to make the most aggressive sounding mix possible.

I pushed up the faders to see what was on the tape. Interestingly, the track had no vocals, just an instrumental – a strange decision, I thought. My normal approach was to start with the drums. I worked to create the kind of drum sounds I liked – a crisp kick with the low end punchy but tight, a snare drum that would cut your ears off with a gated reverb, and tight hi-hats. I only used a minimal amount of the ambient drum sound recorded on two separate tracks as I wanted to make it as controlled and driving as I could.

Next, I made as much of Andy Taylor's guitar parts as possible, making them loud and distorted. Nick's synths were the trademark mixture of chord pads and sequenced pulses, and once again, I made them as aggressive as possible. John's bass originally was in stereo, but not for long, by putting into mono it immediately sat front and centre with the kick drum to create a rhythm section that had punch. I made Duran Duran sound more like an experimental, alternative band than the teen popsters they were known as.

I left Good Earth convinced I would never hear back from them, I don't think I even bothered to name the half inch mixtape, just threw it on the sofa and told the assistant to do with it as he saw fit. I made a cassette, more to play Phil than as any indication of how good it was, and again didn't even name the box other than as DD Mix, which goes a long way to explaining why I'm unsure as to what track it was I actually mixed! In those days before computer recall on mixing desks, where settings could be saved, it was possible and even quite common for people to spend not just hours but even a few days finishing a mix. I knocked this one out in about six hours. "There you go mate, send it on to EMI or whoever."

I drove back to Gallery worrying about how I was going to tell Phil I'd messed up the opportunity he'd created for me. It felt like I'd not been given a fair audition, and that the biggest chance of my fledgling career to date had gone, and I might never have another one even close to it. I told Phil what had happened and plonked myself down on the sofa in the studio's lounge and proceeded to cry like a baby. I played him a copy of the mix and he said nice things about how it sounded more powerful and fresher than some of their previous work, but I wasn't convinced and didn't believe he was either.

Over the following week, much to my complete amazement, the strangest thing happened. One by one, every member of Duran Duran telephoned me to congratulate me on my mix. I think Nick was first, with comments like, that's exactly what we want, a sound that will appeal to an older more mature audience. Andy loved the way I'd featured his guitars so I seemed to have won an ally in him. Without listing the comments of each member, even if I could remember them verbatim, the gist was that they'd never heard their music sound so exciting, so full of energy, and that they would like to work with me on a single, and if that went well then to co-produce the third album with them. After the way I felt on leaving Good Earth that evening, this was a turnaround of epic proportions. I felt vindicated. And it suddenly dawned on me that in truth the mix I created was exactly what they wanted to hear; left to my own devices, they could hear how I'd envisioned their music to sound given a free reign and new creative approach.

I'd got the gig! I was to produce a single for the band, and assuming that went well, the album. To say I was dumbstruck is a given. I jumped up and down on the sofa and yelled for joy, laughing and shouting, "I've done it!"

DURAN DURAN
is there
something I
should know?

7
IS THERE SOMETHING I SHOULD KNOW?

Before I start the story of recording with the band for the first time, I should just sum up my understanding of the band's formative years. I know most of you will know the story, but I think hearing it from me will add some perspective on the events that led up to them deciding to work with me.

Paul and Michael Berrow, the brothers that managed the band at the start of their career, had first recognised not only musical talent in Nick Rhodes and John Taylor, but also how determined they were to succeed. With the addition of Roger Taylor, Andy Taylor and finally Simon Le Bon, Duran Duran were complete. It's amazing how many embryonic bands I came across during my career that had plenty of talent, but lacked the single-mindedness and determination required to make an impression and be disruptive.

Duran Duran's success was far from overnight. The Berrow brothers ran the notorious Rum Runner nightclub in Birmingham, which the band used as a proving ground. During this time, they wrote the songs that were to get them signed and become the first album. The Berrow brothers invested time and money into crafting the band's image, clothes, hair, make up – every aspect of their look was pored over in granular detail. A successful professional photoshoot confirmed that they were ready to face the wider world.

Dave Ambrose at EMI Records was one of the A&R guys who was approached. He signed the band to the label that was once home to The Beatles, the Fab Four. Well now the Fab Five had arrived. Most people think that securing a record deal means you've made it. Actually, it's where the hard work starts, and will often make or break a band.

EMI put the band in the studio with experienced producer Colin Thurston. The eponymous debut album came out in June 1981, reaching the top three in the UK charts and spawning three hit singles – Planet Earth, Careless Memories, and Girls On Film, the latter being a bona fide Top 5 smash hit, propelled by the raunchy Godley & Creme video.

Second album syndrome is such a widely understood phenomenon that it is used as a metaphor outside the craft of music. A lifetime to write and prepare for the debut album, six weeks to write and prepare for the follow-up. As I mentioned in the Preface earlier, Thurston and the band effortlessly pole-vaulted over this notorious career-killer with Rio, including four huge singles – My Own Way, Hungry Like The Wolf, Save A Prayer and the iconic title track. With their US label, Capitol, changing the marketing focus away from new romantic, which was really more of a British fad anyway; and pushing Duran Duran as a dance rock band (including asking established producer David Kershenbaum to remix most of the tracks to sound more appealing to US radio), stateside success followed. The band were now global stars.

Whatever form it took, Duran Duran's third album wouldn't be ready until the end of 1983, a full year after Rio. EMI and the Berrow brothers were concerned that some of the band's commercial momentum would be lost if they were gone from the charts for too long, especially given the famously fickle nature of their target demographic, so there was a sense of urgency. The decision was made to aim for a single around March 1983, to bridge the gap before the arrival of the third album and its own singles.

The sessions to produce what was to become Is There Something I Should Know? started with us all reconvened at Good

Earth, the same studio in a basement in the heart of Soho where I'd created my audition mix. Looking at the steps leading down to the battered door, it was hard to imagine that albums by Thin Lizzy, The Moody Blues, U2, David Bowie, Tina Turner and many more had come from behind that humble portal. Once tea and coffee were in hand, I kicked off by asking to hear the demo of the song we were to record.

Although they had written the songs for their first two albums without outside input, our first day in the studio was pretty much right off the back of the last Rio concert dates. The pressures of touring meant that the third album cycle was starting with no songs yet written. They had a clear concept for the sound they wanted and were famously quoted later as saying they aimed to be a mixture of Chic, Roxy Music and The Sex Pistols.

For many bands, not having finished songs would have created unbearable pressure, but not only did Duran Duran take it in their stride, it would keep things fluid and exciting as the track evolved, especially in the early stages.

So, after setting up, tuning their instruments and warming up, they started to loosely jam together. Andy had a great Beatles-style guitar riff that was hooky and endearing, and it quickly became clear that a song could be built around it. In any situation when a strong musical element was created, the other band members would gravitate towards it regardless of who'd played it first, and ideas would arrive from each of them.

There was plenty of dialogue between us all, and very little argument. We would quickly either approve and incorporate new suggestions, or bin them as unsuitable with no sign of ill will and move on. I was immediately impressed with the calm, democratic approach they adopted at this stage in the new song's early gestation. They had a common sense of purpose, all wanting what was best for the whole. it was obvious to me that the bond between them had played a large part in their success.

I've already mentioned the chemistry between the five members of Duran Duran but haven't explained why it mattered so much. I had many unsigned bands come to me during the years I spent at Gallery, wanting me to produce them. Often the decision was easy. If they couldn't play or didn't have the songs, I declined. In other cases, it was far trickier because they might show promise but it was hard to understand the relationships that existed in the collective. Ultimately, good playing and good songs aren't enough without that magical ingredient, that special level of interaction we call chemistry.

With Duran Duran, it was quickly obvious to me that these five guys, if not psychic (although they did have a habit of finishing each other's sentences), certainly had a clear understanding of what each of them was adding to the whole, which in turn generated mutual respect. This led to a level of trust that stood them in good stead when things became tense or ideas dried up and helped avoid conflict.

Andy's guitar riff was the obvious cornerstone on which to build the track. Once a tempo had been established, a drum machine was used to create a metronomic click, which Roger monitored as he laid down a straightforward beat on the drums that Andy could then play the guitar part to, which became the first part to be recorded, and was kept as finished. Andy was a solid guitarist and generally put his parts down in one or two takes. We might chop between a couple of takes to get the very best version, but in general, he was a breeze to record. If there was room for experimentation, I always found him open to try any ideas suggested.

Even in my short career to that point, I'd already learned that in order to gain a musician's respect, I had to show them that I was not just listening to what they were playing but hearing the subtle nuances of a take and spotting for mistakes. As an example, if John was playing his bass part for the verse, he would play the same phrase over each bar. If I heard one bar that was perfect, I would log the time on the recording machine and then, when he came in to listen back, I would point out the bar where I felt he'd really nailed the phrase. John then knew I was totally tuned in and able to hear the quality of his performance; it was the same with all the band members.

Each person in Duran Duran had their own approach to finding ideas for parts. Nick and Andy would constantly be playing around with various lines and sounds. Roger and John worked together to come up with a solid beat and bass line. All the while, Simon was watching, listening and taking in the development of the track that the others were building. I could almost see his mind running through lyrics or melody lines, trying out ideas as he came up with them. Occasionally he was writing down ideas for lyrics and singing melodies mostly to himself, often barely audible, working with the ever-evolving track.

I was reminded time and again of the advice given to me by Alan Tarney - that when you add a new part to a track, it should lift it in a tangible way. The trend during the early 1980s was to fill the multitrack up with as much stuff as possible, and it took enormous skill to avoid the result becoming a muddy mess, lacking any definition or space. We worked hard looking for parts and sounds that were there for a specific reason.

One of my more enjoyable roles in those early stages was helping Nick find synth sounds that we both felt had something unique about them, whether it was the theatre of a percussive stab, a sequenced line that added to the overall groove, or a pad that created atmosphere and depth.

Nick had an intuitive sense of which sounds worked. His opinions were generally in line with my own. We pored over each of the synths he had and worked through the presets. We found ones we liked then tweaked them to death until we loved it or hated it. With sounds we both liked, Nick would then try playing various lines either of his own creation or suggested by me or members of the band. Regardless of who was making the suggestion, Nick would give each idea a try, and as a group we'd then decide whether it worked. On the very rare occasions when they were all undecided, they would look to me for a deciding vote to resolve a deadlock.

Feeding a sustained synth chord through a noise gate triggered by a rhythmic source (such as a drum machine) creates a rhythmic pulse. Adjusting the gate's frequency, attack and decay makes it possible to shape the way the gate opens and closes to create a pulse that's not quite as hard-edged as a normal synth pulse, more analogue in feel. Roxy Music used this method of creating a repetitive pulse; in their early days, there were no sequencers so it was the only way to create such a part, as physically playing it with metronomic accuracy would be beyond most musicians. Even then, few people were using gates in this way. It's a trick I still use to this day as it creates something unique that harks back to a previous era without sounding dated.

There are a couple of synth parts I'm still particularly fond of. One is a low tone at the end of each four-bar block in the verse. I love the weight it gives the verses combined with Simon's low vocal harmonies, and how it creates a feeling of gravitas. The synth brass sounds still annoy me a bit, but to get a good brass sound from a synth has always been notoriously difficult, especially back then. Nick had a great sense of the dynamics for the song, which was something that helped the arrangement hugely.

Andy, I found to be more self-contained than the other four guys. He knew the sounds he could generate from his guitars and tried out a variety of parts and sounds, alongside the prominent picked riff at the heart of the song. He was a decent rhythm player and tried damped chops; some worked, some didn't. Andy was somewhat unique in the band by having paid his dues before the Duran Duran days, touring with a band across military bases in Europe, making him the most experienced rock 'n' roller of the quintet. At times he was able to draw on that part of his history for inspiration.

Roger and John were a great rhythm section and complemented each other well. For the most part, John's bass would stick to Roger's kick drum, and then he would add counterpoints to drive the beat, with some hard percussive slaps thrown in played with his thumb. Leading up to the chorus he played a simple line in sync with the kick drum then left a note hanging, dropping us right into the chorus.

John never wanted to be a lead guitarist. You'd be surprised how many bass players wish they were lead guitarists and play overly complicated lines that are more suitable as guitar parts. John wasn't one of them. He relished his role creating the weight and rhythmic foundation of the band, working closely with Roger on the beats they crafted. Again – great chemistry which lifted their playing out of the ordinary.

I felt Roger had quite a distinctive style, relatively complex, without ever crossing the line into sounding cluttered. He was already playing a part that fitted the track perfectly, a relatively straight ahead beat with a vibey kick drum pattern that had enough variation to keep your interest. I never had the sense from Roger, or any of the band in fact, that they felt the need to prove themselves to be some amazing virtuoso musician. I liked the way he used tom fills more like instrumental additions as much as percussive ones.

Other than the repeat of the second verse and chorus, there was the addition of the middle eight which focused on Simon's harmonica playing. It was layered and built up around a main theme, bathed in reverb to create an ethereal, otherworldly effect. Roger added a more complex version of the intro kick pattern. John played long, held notes. All the while Andy had fun creating some depth and aggression as well as sustained chords, and Nick's synth pulse helped maintain the groove.

After that, the race through the last choruses to the end of the track. Just about everything moves up a gear. The synth goes up an octave, a trick guaranteed to immediately add excitement. John starts to slap his bass with a more complex part, and Roger switches to double time on the drums creating a more urgent effect. Probably the element providing the most interest is the overlapping of the chorus and verse lyric. Simon sings the main chorus parts and harmonies atop the verse lyrics which are layered with Roger, Andy and John contributing gang vocals. It just grows and grows in excitement to the top of the fade.

Considering we'd started the day with nothing, I was blown away at the rate of progress we were making. I oversaw the performances of each of the guys as they put down their parts but left much of the actual recording to the engineer at Good Earth, preferring to concentrate more on the quality of each performance, looking for any exceptional phrases, or mistakes. My decision to leave the recording to the engineer was one that I was to regret not too long after.

The creative process rarely became bogged down. Throughout the making of the track the ideas continued to flow. I had always felt that one of the most important roles of a producer was to make it as easy as possible for a musician to hear back any idea they'd had as quickly and painlessly as possible in order to maintain the session's momentum. It was always my practice (and one that I'd share with the assistant engineer assigned to each session) to constantly be listening to ideas being discussed and if required, get the sounds being discussed ready to record; or if the focus was something already recorded, have the tape lined up at the right point and the channel open for playback. As an example of the former, if Andy was talking about how his guitar would sound played through a particular amplifier in the live room, I made sure either myself or the assistant went into the live room, mic'd up the amp in question, plugged it through to the desk and allocated a channel to it.

It may never be used, but if Andy suddenly said, hey, let's hear what that amp would sound like, I could just turn on the channel, play the tape and push up the fader. Then he'd hear it as soon as he strummed his guitar. So, instead of there being a coffee break while everything was sorted out, it was all ready to go and the sound could be heard instantly. Little things like that helped keep the momentum of a session flowing. It often meant the difference between a musician being able to express his creativity in the moment or having to wait while technical obstacles were overcome on the way to trying out an idea, that instead of being hot, soon became lukewarm.

The song's creation had proved painless and as I remember there were only a few, rare occasions where we were all stumped as to what was needed next. All of which I repeat because it illustrates once more, more than anything I've said thus far, just how important the chemistry between the five band members was. Without it you are always having to push the river and as anyone who has read Taoist teachings will know, that is a futile exercise. What I mean is that in my opinion the chemistry between the five members of the band was so strong that it enabled them to park their egos and act purely for the good of the whole, not for personal glory. You can imagine how different a task it would be to work with a band lacking that spirit of unity of purpose.

As the track began to sound finished, we started to add accents and points of interest. We'd added big gated reverb sounds on selected snares in the choruses, another trick I'd learned from working with Roxy Music that was very much becoming an 80s sound. You used a long reverb to the snare but then employed a noise gate to cut it off precisely in time to run perfectly into the next kick drum. It creates a great addition to the impact of certain snare hits but without drowning out the rest of the track and can help the beat roll. It has a real impact. Listen for it and you'll hear the difference it makes, even though we used the effect sparingly.

It was all coming together, so far, so good. During the writing stage with Roger and John, I didn't feel they needed much advice, although they looked to me for feedback, which of course I happily provided. Once everyone's parts were worked out, I concentrated on their performances as they were recorded. I listened for mistakes, as well as the perfect bar.

Andy worked out most of his parts before he started and was almost always spot on after a couple of takes. Alan Tarney again: once you have the chord structure in place and are starting to build the track up, you should hear plenty of parts, counterpoints or layers. It shouldn't be a struggle, and if it is, the chances are the chord progressions themselves are not good enough. Priceless advice that can and probably did save hours of fruitless work.

Throughout the sessions, Simon was a constant presence as I previously noted. He was usually sitting in a corner somewhere, notebook in hand, jotting down ideas for lyrics. I later found out more about how Simon liked to work up an idea until he felt confident enough to try putting down either a guide or an early attempt at a master vocal, depending how he felt about the progress he'd made. Having a strong melodic and lyrical pattern, especially for the chorus, seemed to give him the confidence to tackle the lead vocal. He'd la-di-da through the structure of the song, and as its shape became solidified and he knew how the verse flowed into the chorus, he would start to come up with more ideas for melody lines that fitted over the musical shape of each section. He knew he had to tell a story with the verses, however oblique, and that the chorus needed a repeatable motif that contained, in most cases, the song's title and main hook. This was not always the case, but a good rule of thumb.

An issue for Simon was that if nothing on a track really defined his melodic line, he would sometimes struggle a bit. In some cases, where the backing track was very bare, like some of today's highly rhythmic R&B or, say, Prince's songs on Sign O' The Times, and there was very little melodic activity to pitch a melody against, Simon would be lost. He needed something like a pad to which he could link. I can't sing to save my life, so the fact that he could pull himself close enough to be acceptable was amazing. That's not an easy thing to do. I don't think he lacked objectivity in terms of his own output, and I don't think he would have been at all musical if he couldn't hear his own limitations, but one of the things about Simon as a person was that he didn't want to show any sort of vulnerability, so he'd never come into the control room after a take and say "Wow, am I out of tune!" Instead he'd go "Cool, how's that?" He'd always try to put a positive spin on it, and yet if you said, "Simon, go and do it again", there was never a problem. He was realistic and always up for it with a positive attitude.

As the verse lyric grew alongside a melodic line, he'd start trying out his vocals, almost singing to himself as the track was played through and other parts were being laid down. It was obvious to me that Simon really understood the importance of having a hooky chorus, both lyrically and melodically, and spent plenty of time working on ideas for those sections. Working on our first song together as a team, Simon's part arrived pretty much on cue. The bulk of the instrumental tracks having been recorded, we'd reached the point where the only major thing left to be completed was his vocals.

Simon's vocal session was as smooth and straightforward as any that I'd recorded to date. After the odd word change and phrasing adjustment, we had a master lead vocal done, and were onto looking for sections to double up - or where harmonies would add depth and interest. Although I'd heard he sometimes could have trouble hitting pitch, he didn't seem to have any problems that we couldn't tweak with effects like an Eventide harmoniser, and some reverb that had the effect of sitting the vocal comfortably into the track, giving it context.

I was most impressed with his phrasing. He seemed able to really tell the story of the lyrics by his emphasis on certain lines. I was genuinely relieved and somewhat moved. It sounded great. The low harmonies, almost groans, that appear in the second verse, are amongst my favourite vocal parts. His other doubles and harmonies were not too complicated, often a problem with many singers who feel they need to add the proverbial kitchen sink into the arrangement. Simon was happy to do enough to just put the icing on the cake. In the end it all seemed to hang together well. As a producer you always want to try and improve little things. But at some point, you must accept that's it, and to put in more time and effort would only result in diminishing returns. After adding a few little sound effects and dynamic accents, all was well.

One final part was the intro. I felt that starting with Andy's guitar was too much like many other songs and that we needed something dramatic to announce its arrival, so that the second time anyone heard it they'd instantly know it was Duran Duran's new single. They agreed, and I suggested we try to do something like the start of Be My Baby by The Ronettes, an old Motown classic. It had a dramatic drumbeat (boom, ba-boom CRASH!) which Roger easily picked up and played, while Simon sang "Please please tell me now". And that's the intro the whole world knows. I thought it sounded great and added the right sort of impact that the first single of the band's new era needed. We had our song.

Phil Thornalley Alamy

8

MIXING
IS THERE SOMETHING I SHOULD KNOW?

The journey had been a joy to be part of. It very quickly became obvious to me that contrary to the initial rumours of Duran Duran being a puppet band, constructed and produced with little or no input of their own, they knew exactly what they were doing, and were fully aware of the high standards they needed to maintain. I was impressed and loving every minute. The guys were great to be around, they knew they were flying high on their amazing journey and I felt incredibly privileged to be part of it.

We were ready to start mixing the track to create a finished record. All the time while you're recording the various parts that make up a song, you are balancing the levels of each musical element as you go, edging towards an approximation of the sound of the finished record.

I had been involved, like the rest of the band, right from the beginning and was starting to find it hard to hear the wood from the trees, making it difficult to retain the kind of objectivity needed to mix a track effectively. You know all the parts intimately so it's difficult to judge what level each should be at to be audible. You know every element that's on the multitrack so it's easy to hear them even when the whole thing's a swamp – but a first-time listener would be baffled.

We booked more time at Good Earth and reconvened after a short break to start mixing. Mixing had always been one of my favourite aspects of creating recorded music, it's a bit like cooking an exotic dish. If recording is a process of choosing and blending all the ingredients, mixing is where you throw it all in the pan and make it stick.

However, the ingredients of Is There Something I Should Know? curdled in the pan. Nothing gelled. I was frustrated and baffled. It didn't matter how many times we tried to balance the track. To leave the cooking analogy behind and move to athletics, every combination would trip on one hurdle or another. We'd set up a mix which sounded right at the start, but when the track reached the chorus, the drums were too low. So, we'd naturally lift their volume but then when we returned to the start, they were far too loud. We, or more accurately I, just couldn't find a balance that worked throughout the track. I was completely mystified. All I could think of was that it was because I wasn't familiar with Good Earth's loudspeakers, known in pro studios as monitors. After several failed attempts, I expressed my concerns about Good Earth's monitors and suggested we go to Gallery, where I'd worked for over three years at that point. I felt that as I knew the sound in the studio more intimately, it would be easier to create a solid mix there.

We took the multitrack down to Chertsey in Surrey and I got to work on the desk I had used every day for three years. Alas, Gallery betrayed me as surely as Good Earth had done. It just sounded plain wrong. I was starting to panic. Was I out of my depth? My ideas were good, but was my technical ability lacking? To say I was starting to become concerned would be an understatement and worse, I could sense that the band were beginning to have their doubts about my ability as well. Sure, we'd created the track and I'd certainly done a good job as co-producer, working well with the five members of the band, acting like a lightning rod to channel their ideas onto tape and incorporate them into the ever-evolving track. I'd understood the chemistry between each of them and made sure they all performed to the best of their abilities. I heard every nuance of their performances, using my ability to really focus in on each note and bar, and as such had won their respect.

We were all happy when we left Good Earth for a short break before starting the final mix, but between those sessions and the mix it was almost as if something had happened to the recordings, surely it shouldn't be this hard to mix the song? Certainly, it was an ambitious track, but I'd worked on plenty of works of similar or greater complexity with Roxy Music amongst others, so it was a bit of a mystery. One of the band members suggested going to Eel Pie Studio, a unique facility owned by The Who's lead guitarist Pete Townsend. I'd never worked there before, but it turned out to be a superb place. It was built on a small island in the middle of the River Thames in Twickenham, west of Central London. Unfortunately, more of the same problems; we just could not find a balance that worked from beginning to end of the song.

In desperation, and almost as a last resort, I suggested we go to New York and ask Bob Clearmountain to tame this beast. It would be an expensive undertaking but at this point EMI, the Berrows, the band and not least myself needed to get the damn thing finished. It was agreed, and we set off for the Big Apple and The Power Station.

Watching Clearmountain work in between jet lag-induced naps was a sight to behold. If you could insure a pair of ears, his would have been covered for many millions. He heard subtleties and nuances that would go straight over the head of even the most experienced engineer, musician or producer. I was watching a master at work. The mix he produced was undoubtedly gorgeous. But once back in London the consensus was that it just wasn't the right sound for a Duran Duran record. Although Clearmountain had balanced the track well and created some beautiful sounds, overall the general view was that it sounded more like a guitar-based band and lacked that mix of synths and guitars that previous Duran Duran records had exhibited. With hindsight it's easy to see how he approached the mix, which was to make it as musical as possible, focusing on Andy's guitar riff and keeping Nick's synths much lower in the mix than originally intended. He'd made it sound more like an FM radio track that wouldn't have sounded out of place several years earlier. Another failure. I was now teetering on the very tip of the plank I'd been walking along since my first attempts at Good Earth failed.

I can't remember who came up with the idea, but the suggestion was made that we go to Alex Sadkin, an American producer based in London working primarily out of RAK studios in St John's Wood, close to Abbey Road Studios. Alex had a long and superb track record, having started out working for Island Records' founder Chris Blackwell at Compass Point in the Bahamas, where he had the brilliant idea of combining Grace Jones' unique appearance and vocal style with reggae's best rhythm section, Sly & Robbie. A trio of classic albums came from this inspired hook up between 1980 and 1982: Warm Leatherette, Nightclubbing and Living My Life. All of them are well worth checking out, especially for their immaculate production. Most recently, he was fresh from producing Quick Step & Side Kick for The Thompson Twins which had managed the feat of becoming a big record in the United States, a formula Duran Duran hoped to emulate.

Despite having a heavy schedule, Alex agreed to tackle the mix without much convincing, Duran Duran already being one the biggest bands in the UK and Europe. Alex and his superbly talented engineer Phil Thornalley quickly identified the problem. They pointed out that the levels of individual drums were inconsistent, they came and went as you listened to the mix; one minute you could hear them perfectly well, the next they were lost amongst the other sounds. As later became apparent, this was because I'd been naïve enough to leave the recording of the drums to the assistant engineer at Good Earth and he had lacked the engineering skills to be able to use compressors and limiters well enough to be able to record the drums at a consistent level. This explained why we couldn't get a balance that worked throughout all sections of the song; they might be loud enough during the verses when the track was quite empty, but would then be too quiet when the choruses came along and the tracks were much fuller with far more parts competing for space. In the end it was so simple but had taken Alex's vast experience to spot the problem at all.

Samplers were still at least a year in the future, but there was a device called a DMS digital delay that enabled you to capture a sound and then have it triggered by an external sound on the same principle as the noise gate we used to create the synth pulse on the chorus. Instead of opening and closing a noise gate, the DMS would trigger the sample. Phil used graphic equalisers on each individual channel to reduce all the recorded drum sounds to tightly compressed clicks, making them ideal as triggers. We hired a stack of DMS machines and Phil then loaded his and Alex's favourite drum sounds.

When they pressed play on the tape machine and played the track, instead of hearing the acoustic drum kit, we had perfect, loud, crisp, consistent drums, each note perfect, but retaining Roger's live feel and groove. This was a massive relief for everyone but especially for me. The track sounded brilliant, the drums were pumping as intended, Alex and Phil must have thought they'd just played midwives to expectant parents! Our baby was born, and it was perfect, just as it should be.

Once the drums were in place, we added John's bass to the mix, and on solid foundations at last, the rest of the track was built up from there. Alex and Phil were an amazing pair, they had the same kind of almost telepathic understanding that the band had. It made the mixing process a real joy to behold. After several hours of work, the record you've all come to love and enjoy was finished. After each previous failure I'd felt more than a little worried if we would be able to finally deliver the single to EMI and the Berrows; however we were all confident that it was at last ready to be manufactured and released to the millions of fans waiting for this stand-alone single, a track that was going to have to keep them going until the album. It came so close to never happening but Is There Something I Should Know? was released in the UK on 14 March 1983.

Back then, the charts were compiled by Gallup, an American analytics company, who took sales data from a sample of around 300 record shops across the country, known as chart return shops. The shops' identity was a closely guarded secret, although known to the reps who sold stock in from the major labels. In fact, even to a keen-eyed customer it was usually obvious if they were in a chart return shop because limited edition versions of new releases (bonus poster, coloured vinyl, sometimes a bonus record known as the elusive 'double pack'), rare as rocking horse shit elsewhere, were all generously stocked. The new chart would be announced to the record companies on Tuesday evening by Gallup. The week after Is There Something I Should Know? was released, the band and myself convened back at Good Earth studios to wait for the call from EMI, to tell us what position the single had entered the chart.

The Berrows were there and it was Paul who took the call. He wouldn't have made a very good poker player as we could tell as soon as he heard our chart entry - a beaming grin spread across his face. We'd gone in at number one! NUMBER ONE! We went mad, hugging each other, squealing with excitement. This also meant that the following week's edition of Top Of The Pops would feature Duran Duran in that coveted last slot when the presenter would close the show by saying "And now, this week's brand-new number one, Duran Duran!" Unreal, anyone starting out in music production or creation dreams of such moments, whether they like to admit it or not, and it had happened. We all ran upstairs from Good Earth's basement and across the street into the nearest pub where me and several of the band then realised we hadn't got any cash with us, so it came down to the Berrows to get the celebratory drinks in.

It really wasn't until I got back to Gallery and saw Phil that it all started to sink in, the fact that I'd produced the UK's number one single, that my name would appear in the credits listed in the UK trade magazine Music Week as co-producer alongside the band, and would also appear in the US equivalent Billboard, which listed the UK charts as well as their own.

In the US, Is There Something I Should Know? topped out at number four, not bad considering the previous single Rio had only reached the Top 20 over there, and number nine in the UK. To have your name attached to a number one single is not something that happens to everyone and something I will always be proud of, along with the success of The Reflex and several other songs.

Although it was to become quite commonplace for major bands to enter at number one - as record companies put more and more of their promotional efforts into the pre-release campaign, stoking anticipation and getting as many sales in the first week to give a single the prestige of a high chart entry - at that the time of Is There Something I Should Know? we were only something like the fourteenth record to have pulled off that feat since the charts had started.

Although it was a stand-alone single that never appeared on a studio album, Is There Something I Should Know? appeared (somewhat out of place I feel) on the Capitol re-release of the eponymous debut album in the States; and has of course appeared on every official greatest hits compilation they've released, one of only two UK number one singles for the band.

Kathmandu

9

IAN LITTLE
THE EARLY YEARS

Before I write about the creation of Seven And The Ragged Tiger I want to give you a little breather; tell you something about myself, the path I'd been on before I started working with the architects who gave me my first taste of the music industry. I want to do this so you have a better understanding of the dynamics between me and the band, and also to put into context just what a massive step up it was for me to end up working with this amazing group as they reached the peak of their powers.

I was orphaned at birth and adopted by a loving, Christian family when I was just a six-month-old baby. My adoptive father was ex Royal Navy and my mum a housewife. I had a wonderfully happy childhood. There was no information about my biological parents, but that never bothered me, in fact it made it easier for me to accept things as they were. My parents were simply my parents. Dad died when I was just eleven. My mum, however, lived to be eighty, despite suffering a stroke at sixty.

My loving parents were brilliant. I wanted for nothing, in a three-bed semi-detached house in Hamsey Green, a hamlet attached to the village of Sanderstead east of Purley in Surrey, five miles south of Croydon. Before I reached the age of ten and was still full of the sense of wonder of discovering life, the thing I feared most was the ordinary. Like most children I wanted to cross any boundary and push against limits my parents or authorities created. Anything average, sensible or normal seemed to represent a life of grey boredom. I don't know how much I understood about my desire to break out of the restraints of a class-riddled society back then, but I did know I was ambitious (even if at that time it was to become a racing driver). I started to do whatever I could to free myself from the normality of my life as quickly as possible. I later realised my life during those years was far from typical.

Sadly, because my dad died after a prolonged illness when I was still young, I had little time to really know him. The memories I do have, before he became terminally ill, were of someone that loved me and made every effort to make my life as enjoyable as he could. He had a Mini company car that he used to drive fast, faster than mum liked, and I can remember him catching my eye in the rear-view mirror and winking at me as mum complained. Precious gems.

My mum remarried an old friend of our family, but my relationship with my stepdad was always rocky. As I became older, I realised my mum had only remarried to keep our family home together.

The class system is still entrenched in British culture. It was even more prevalent in the 1960s, as I entered my early teens. Britons knew their station in life and acted accordingly. The titled classes ruled. Going to the right schools and universities was prerequisite to a fast track into positions of wealth and power. This slowly changed during the latter part of the last century and permeates society less now. Back then, all us ordinary folk were aware of people that lived in huge stately homes, set in grounds the size of a large park. Despite knowing of their existence, we knew nothing about the actual nature of their lifestyles. Instead, we believed in the way their lives were portrayed in TV dramas or the movies.

Fleeting glimpses of families who had servants didn't give ordinary people a real understanding of how these wealthy individuals actually lived. The reality of how the super-rich behaved remained hidden. Most people couldn't imagine what it would be like to have such material wealth. Like trained lab rats, people become accustomed to having a certain amount of space to live in, so many weeks holiday a year, and other materialistic metrics that combine to define their standard of living.

There are parallels to the story of Buddha's first experience of people living outside the world of plenty he knew, and his subsequent total inability to understand why these people had nothing. The same might have been true during the era of master and servants. Thanks to the deep-rooted sense of place this perverse relationship created, the lower classes accepted their position in life, however demeaning.

Sometimes, as a kid knowing I was adopted, if I was in trouble and sent to my room, I'd imagine my 'real' parents arriving in a Rolls Royce to drive me off to my country mansion. Naturally, I never thought it through. I never considered the pain of leaving my adoptive (but actual) parents and other practical considerations that tend to be overlooked in such fantasies. The point is, I felt I belonged in that wealthy world. Not so much the realm of blue-blooded aristocrats, but people at the top of their game, successful and wealthy as a result. I was driven and ambitious.

The teenage me didn't understand the full ramifications of these feelings. I was aware of the difference between being a worker or a boss. Right from my earliest memories, important decisions made in my life were designed to make it possible for me to achieve more. Even going to university rather than doing an apprenticeship created a way of putting me in the right place to meet people of influence able to present me with opportunities that would have otherwise passed me by.

By the age of twelve, I became interested in the growing hippie culture in London and sought out copies of underground papers like Oz and the International Times. I read about grass and hashish as well as the thing that intrigued me most, LSD-25, the original compound first discovered by Albert Hoffman in April 1943. In 1968, on my fourteenth birthday, I smoked my first spliff of hashish and loved it. A year or so earlier my friends and I had started drinking, but I didn't like the taste of alcohol or its effects and would down a bottle of Southern Comfort as quickly as possible, just to get drunk, and I was usually very sick soon after. Dope, on the other hand, suited me perfectly. I quickly realised how much more I heard in the music I loved, and how my experience of life and the arts was simply more intense. Being stoned, I was able to really focus intently on whatever I was into. My experience of life was richer, more detailed and insightful.

Most of my school friends were forced into law or medicine by high pressure parenting, anything that would help them earn a decent salary, regardless of whether their hearts were into it or not. My mum was different; she appreciated the value of being happy and content. She understood that was only possible if you chose a path your heart was in.

The first time this manifested itself in a life changing way was when, after already securing an engineering apprenticeship at Porsche and in my final year at high school, my art master asked me which art schools I'd applied for. When I revealed that I hadn't, but was going to go to Porsche, he had the wisdom to give me a massive wake up call. He pointed out that the only reason I was going to work for Porsche was because I wanted to be a racing driver, having been a go-kart racer since I was twelve, and that in reality I'd end up as an engineer instead.

Although there's certainly nothing wrong with being an engineer, he made it clear that it probably wasn't what I actually wanted and that going to university was in itself a life-changing experience, regardless of the subject. No one in my family had ever been to university. I would be the first. The only subject I was anywhere near good enough to take a degree in was fine art, something that hadn't been overlooked by my art teacher. He knew that having planted the idea of going to university, we had a year for me to pass the necessary school leaving exams, known as A-Levels, required to apply for a place. At least one A-Level pass (grade C or higher) was a prerequisite to applying for a place on a degree course.

During my time at art school, I learned about perception, the relationship between perceiver and perceived, how my senses worked, and how to focus and develop the level of detail I saw. I realised that it's almost as if there's a volume control on the intensity with which you perceive anything. On the one hand you can glance across the front page of a newspaper, just taking in the headlines, almost unconsciously or study the text in detail and gain an in-depth understanding of what has been written. It's a bit like the difference between seeing a flock of birds or observing the minute markings on the back of a ladybird. This realisation that there are many different levels of perception was a real epiphany for me. I saw the riches in great paintings and perceived myself and the world around me in a more detailed and intense fashion.

Whilst at art school, I also became fascinated by all forms of spiritual teachings from various sources ranging from simple yoga, the huge main religions of the world, to many, far more obscure groups. Some, particularly in India, centred around the utterances of a single individual, some still living.

This combination of gradually understanding the process of perception and how I saw the universe - as well as the image I had of myself, paired with practicing meditation and studying spiritual texts - helped lead me towards a path to finding truth. In 1972, at age 18, I was a classic late-adopter hippie and had already taken a lot of LSD-25.

Tom Wolf's 1968 seminal book The Electric Kool-Aid Acid Test chronicles parties in which LSD-laced Kool-Aid was used for a communal trip and the group's encounters with well-known figures of the time including famous authors, Hell's Angels and The Grateful Dead, and Kesey's exile to Mexico. My own experience meshed with theirs. LSD has the capacity to give you a glimpse of the oneness of all things. Even though drug-induced and temporary, the understanding and insights I gained through those experiences instilled in me a freedom and inner contentment that has seen me survive what has been a rollercoaster of a life.

Whilst I write in a positive light about my experiences, I need to point out two things. Firstly, I don't know if it is even possible to obtain LSD-25 anymore. Secondly, and just as important, it was as much about the time and place as it was the purity of the drug itself. I would never advocate the use of any drugs that you don't confidently know the chemical composition of, or if taken, prevent you from doing what you needed to accomplish in life. I would never advocate drug use any more than I would advocate excessive consumption of alcohol.

Fabulous Furry Freak Brothers Compendium

Rian Huges & Rip Off Press

10
THE PERFECTION OF BEING

In case you think all that follows in this chapter is all hippy BS, here is a quote from American Neurologist David Eagleman, a well-respected scientist who has studied the human brain for over twenty years.

"Who's in control of what you do? It sounds like a simple question; but the facts might surprise you. Almost every action that you take, every decision that you make, and every belief that you hold, these are driven by parts of your brain that you have no access to. We call this hidden world the unconscious, and it runs much more of your life than you'd ever imagine."

To complete your picture and understanding of me and the values that have enabled me to remain at peace and contentment during a life of extremes, I want to describe several experiences that occurred over a period of some twenty years on three different continents that changed my life. To describe the first of these, we have to go back to 1974/5 and an amazing journey I went on six months after leaving art school.

My girlfriend at the time and I both wanted to travel to India, and on into southeast Asia via Nepal. Through a quirk of cheap flights, our trip would also include a short stay in Bangladesh. We wanted to end up in Australia, find work, and make enough to go back and spend more time in India on our way home. We'd met a German couple who were buying genuinely old Tibetan jewellery and artefacts and taking them back to Europe to sell for a huge mark up. They were making enough money in two trips to live the rest of the year in India in some comfort. We intended on doing the same.

Before we could start our trip, we needed work visas for Australia. To obtain those we had to show we each had £150 for every month we wanted to stay. Having far less than required for our aim of a six month stay, I put all my money into my girlfriend's bank account, adding to her own funds, and got a statement. Then she did the same for me. We then applied for and obtained the visas we needed. As an aside, when we eventually reached Perth almost 18 months later, we had $50 between us and were petrified that the customs people would ask us for some proof of having access to the huge sums we claimed to have. Much to our relief, nothing was said. Instead the customs officials were more concerned that we weren't bringing some dangerous critters or drugs into their country secreted in our backpacks.

We left London with about £600 each, with plans to be in Asia for as long as possible. We bought one-way tickets to Delhi via Amsterdam with an unscheduled stop in Kabul, Afghanistan. This stop was due to passengers near one of the rear doors hearing a loud hissing sound, suggesting a leak in the jetliner's pressurised cabin!

We disembarked and were led across the grass beside the runway to an area outside the main buildings where we were told to just sit around, as we watched the local ground crew's attempts at fixing the problem. This involved them pushing a shaky looking bamboo scaffold (bear in mind just how big a jumbo jet is!) up to the guilty door, which they then started opening and closing with increasing force. We could hear plenty of hammering and banging as they worked for about an hour to fix things. After having seemingly made little impression on the faulty door, we were ushered back onto the plane and were soon on our way for the short trip onwards to Delhi. The hissing noise continued, causing several concerned looks towards the offending door, which was sounding more and more like a kettle on the boil.

We landed safely at our destination and the door was soon forgotten, although when the wheels were extended on approach some passengers seated near us burst into tears, which made me think the loud noise was a further degradation of the plane's mechanical integrity (but was in fact their joy at their imminent homecoming).

Upon exiting the terminal, we were determined to start as we meant to continue, using local amenities and spending as little money as possible, and so we immediately looked for some form of public transport. We needed to get to the centre of Delhi, then find the old part of town and suitable cheap accommodation.

My first culture shock in India came as we approached the buses. They had no windows down the sides and were brightly painted top to bottom with images of Hindu deities and festooned with strings of beads and other things that looked a bit like Christmas decorations.

The driver looked like he should still be at school and was wearing no more than a simple loin cloth. As we made our way towards the heart of this sprawling metropolis after sunset, the streets were lit up by open fires set on the pavements, around which groups of men and boys sat animatedly discussing the matters of the day. I can remember that ride as if it were yesterday. Some memories seem to be etched into my consciousness with laser-like precision and have stayed with me ever since. That journey and our subsequent search for a cheap place to stay navigating the timeless bazaars of old Delhi are among those.

We travelled across northern India to Agra, home of the Taj Mahal. Then, all on local trains and buses, we made a 24-hour trip up to the border with western Nepal. The capital of this magical kingdom was Kathmandu. The old part of the city was like going back several hundred years. Dark heavy wooden structures were a mixture of temples and palaces, giving a real sense of the timeless traditions that underlined the culture of this ancient Himalayan kingdom. Incredibly detailed carved columns and recessed panels meant I easily became totally immersed in the atmosphere these mysterious buildings created.

By this point in our journey we were old hands at using local accommodation that we always sought out in order to spend as little money as possible. All we looked for was a rope bed and a wooden door with bolts on the inside and padlocks on the outside. The windows were usually without glass.

One evening in Kathmandu we were out having dinner when I suddenly felt as if I was about to start a full-blown LSD-25 episode. The only thing was, I hadn't taken any, not even any hashish, so it was even more disorientating. I immediately stood up, unable to talk, and ran out of the restaurant. It's almost impossible to describe how I felt. The closest I can come is to ask you to imagine being overwhelmed by white noise and white light. All boundaries were dissolving, the distinction between me and the world around me fading into a grid of energy. As if guided by an internal sat nav, I somehow managed to make my way back to our room, unlock the padlock, push open the door and collapse on the bed.

I was floating around in an ever-evolving machine that seemed to be alive. Neither at the time or in later years have I ever understood what it was. All that mattered was that at its centre was a brilliant light. I wasn't afraid, this light was a manifestation of pure unconditional love and I was drawn towards it. I understood, prior to tangible thoughts, that the light was the portal between this world and the next, and the desire to merge with it was compelling. It seemed to represent the oneness of all things. It was clear that this was a glimpse of truth, and nothing to fear.

At this point my friends returned and I can remember my girlfriend screaming "He's grey, he's grey!" Unable to talk or move, I was able to wiggle a finger or foot, something to show I was still alive, and it became almost instantly clear to me that this was not my time to go into the light, to die, and in an instant I was back in the room. The episode was over. I slowly regained control of my body and gradually sat up and looked around. Everything was the same but totally transformed. It's difficult to describe, but from the bare bulb hanging from the ceiling to the faces of my worried friends, everything was sparkling, glowing, and all I could feel was love.

Although the memory was so fresh, as soon as I tried to describe what I'd just been through in words they just made it seem like a special effects-loaded movie. Nonetheless it had changed me forever, my friends could sense it, and I had direct knowledge of it. People who have taken LSD-25 describe having flashbacks but I don't really think this was one of those episodes. I'd had an insight into what happens when death occurs and it is clearly a kind of homecoming. The light I was so tempted to merge with was pure love. Nothing to fear. The allure of the light was testament to that truth.

When I talk about direct knowledge, understanding opposed to intellectual comprehension, a good analogy to explain the difference is the story of a king, who, having never encountered one before, wanted to know what a mango was. He called his three wisest men and asked them to explain what this new fruit was. The first talked of the texture, the second of its aroma and juiciness. But the third just presented the king with a mango and said, "Here your highness, take a bite." At once the king knew what a mango was – through direct experience.

So it is with truth, once you glimpse it you know, you understand that truth is the oneness of all things. My near-death experience gave me that glimpse of the oneness of all things and throughout the rest of my life I have practiced meditation, and tried to remain in the moment, as it is only in the here and now that I can experience the perfection and completeness of life.

People are analogous to computers; our personalities are like the programmes and our essence is akin to electricity. Sadly, especially in the Western world, our society has grown around the development of personality and the acquisition of material wealth, at the expense of awareness of our essence, and so by the time we have grown from innocent babies into young children we have already lost contact with our essence and identify only with our personalities. Identifying with your personality is the same as thinking you are the programmes running on a computer, at death it will simply dissolve and dissipate. Whereas if your sense of self is identified with your essence, death is the great liberation, allowing you to merge with that light, that pure unconditional love.

Think about how you make decisions. Your choices are based on your tastes and values, your likes and dislikes, which have evolved during your lifetime. They are a mixture of nature and nurture. In other words, your personality is partly genetic, partly the result of the influences you were exposed to as you grew up. The thing is, you had no say in either of those major influences. To take back control requires being present in the moment, of being in the here and now.

If, after reading this, you find you have any interest in the experiences I went through and remember, I am by no means alone. There are many books recounting the experiences of countless people who have had similar near death episodes, either on operating tables or some other life threatening episode, and although the language and circumstances may vary, most talk about having experienced the truth at the heart of all life manifesting as a welcoming light. The light is always recognised as the portal between this world and the next. We can make the transition from our sense of being a separate entity, to merging with the light that is at the heart of and ultimately is everything.

Just to put my experiences into context, every one of you will have experienced the truth, although you might not have recognised it for what it really was. Those moments when the sun is shining; you're with the person or people you love, and all seems right with the world. What I'm talking about is having that feeling as your default state, all the time, whatever the conditions may be around you. And believe me it is within your grasp, with the practice of meditation, yoga, tai chi, simple contemplation, a stilling of the mind to allow the peace within to shine through.

The key is whether your sense of self is identified with your essence or your personality, and whether you know with your intellect or as the result of direct experience, prior to thought, like the king tasting the mango. The important thing about understanding that comes about through direct experience is that it is seated in your essence, not the intellect. As such, it brings with it the sense of oneness that dispels the illusion that we are each separate, isolated entities.

My experience in Nepal had the effect of giving me an unshakable understanding, prior to thought, of the perfection of the moment, the here and now. That direct knowledge of the truth is at the heart of living life in a state of bliss and freedom from fear. Having an insight into the nature of the transition from life to death took away any lingering fear I still had towards my own mortality. With that knowledge came an underlying peace and contentment that remains as my state or 'default setting' to this day. Having said that, I cannot claim to always be in The moment. Like all people, I often find myself lost in my thoughts and not aware of the wind touching my skin or the sun on my face. Thankfully, after years of practice, I now find I soon return to the present moment and the peace that brings.

When we are lost in thought, we either go back into the past and recall memories of happier times or experience regrets about mistakes we've made, things that we can do nothing to change. Or we project into the future, again either anticipating pleasures to come or worrying about problems we expect to face, usually at times when we can do nothing about them, like when trying to sleep. Our minds are powerful, we have incredible imaginations, and can create monsters out of future challenges that not even Superman could tackle. Whereas if we live in the moment, when those problems are our reality, you will find that we have far more capacity to deal with them than expected. Put bluntly, we either deal with the problem or it will become a major problem that ends up in our demise! In most cases we overcome each problem and continue our lives. As with setting goals, there is nothing wrong with planning ahead and making sure we are as prepared to deal with problems when they arise, but there is nothing to be gained by constantly revisiting the matter until it needs dealing with.

For those of you reading this that have no knowledge of yoga or any spiritual teachings, you may find it all a bit far-fetched and may be wondering what any of this chapter has to do with Duran Duran. The reason I am sharing my experiences and understanding with you is because I've had an incredible life that has not always been what most people would consider successful. Yet throughout I've remained, in large part, happy, content and at peace.

As an example of these epiphanies not being reliant on some exotic or idyllic place, the next of my three revelations was very different. It didn't involve a near-death encounter, but was still an experience that affected me profoundly.

After arriving in Perth following our travels in Asia, we spent a few weeks looking for work and I secured a brilliant job working at the local fruit and vegetable market. I worked three late shifts helping unload the grower's trucks as they delivered their wares to the market. Then I would have to come in the following three mornings at the crack of dawn to oversee the sale of the boxes and boxes of produce.

Reaching the market involved me walking about a mile or so along the edge of a highway. One morning, as I walked along with these massive trucks thundering past me, the sun was starting to show itself above the horizon. It was a beautiful yellow-orange hue. I was present, yet in a flash, was taken back to that feeling of being immersed in light and totally as one with the universe. It was incongruous and at odds with my surroundings, but struck me so forcefully that I was forced to stop and just stare at the sun as it slowly rose in the morning sky. I was present, in the moment, and again had a profound experience of perfection. Here was confirmation of all that I'd learned, all the understanding I'd gained through direct knowledge and the experiences I'd had along the way during my still-short life. Here and now lies perfection. To look for it elsewhere is futile and only leads to misery and discontent.

My third direct experience of the truth involved a second near-death encounter that occurred many years later, after the events that make up the bulk of this book. In 1989, I moved to New York. After several happy and successful years, the goals I had set myself on arriving in the United States all fell apart over a period of about ten days. I relapsed into drug abuse. I lost the love of my life and my business. Three months later I tried to take my own life. I injected a gram of cocaine bought from a Spanish 'grocery' store opposite my expensive apartment block.

This time the experience was rather different. Mainlining (injecting a substance directly into your bloodstream) that amount of cocaine meant that I was not lying on the wooden floor of the apartment, I was bouncing off it as my body convulsed, my heart stopping and starting. I bit into my tongue and I could 'see' my body was covered in horrible black, giant beetle-like creatures who were all chomping at my flesh. It was a nightmare but I was conscious, even if in a very strange state. I felt every bite that they were making into my skin.

I realised that I didn't want to die. The only way I could survive this horror was to go into deep meditation and try to connect with my essence. As soon as I identified with my breath, rising and falling within, all was peace. But if my attention was caught by a thought, or train of thought, even for a second, the nightmare returned. I went deeper and deeper into identifying with myself and then the light appeared. Again, I knew it was pure, unconditional love. The urge to merge with the light was as strong as the first time in Nepal, but once again I knew it wasn't the time for me to leave this world. On this occasion, it was mainly because of the suffering it would have caused my mum, who was still alive. I also gained an understanding of why committing suicide is wrong and even considered a sin in some religions. It struck me like a flash as being the ultimate arrogance, by in effect saying to this amazing gift that is life, "Thanks, but no thanks!"

These experiences don't last forever. What's left behind is an underlying sense of peace and contentment that has remained with me ever since. Sometimes it's my predominant state of being. At others it's just bubbling under the surface. I've yet to manage to stay in the here and now continuously in the everyday hustle and bustle of normal life. But when I start to follow and identify with my thoughts, I usually return to being in the moment again quite quickly and certainly before I'm lost in thought for long enough to seriously affect my mood.

Those of you willing to seek and embrace spiritual change are part of a small but growing group of spiritual pioneers striving to reach a point where they can break free of their previously preconditioned state of mind and accept the perfection of the moment.

In the same way as things I read in my teens (that I possibly didn't fully understand at the time) have become the bedrock of my inner strength, I hope that some of the thoughts I've shared here may one day help you.

It all comes down to one simple fact; that if you accept each moment as being perfect, if for no other reason than it IS your current reality, you will be at Peace and Content. I think you'd agree that is a better starting point towards improving things than being dissatisfied and unhappy. To want this moment to be different, is futile. You may think that I'm suggesting you can't do anything to improve your standard of living or have ambition. I'm not. There's nothing wrong with setting goals, wanting more out of life and striving to be the best you can be.

An objection I often hear in response to the statement that Now is Perfect is that apart from their own lives not being as they'd like, people point out that there are many individuals (in fact whole communities) whose lives are desperate through lack of food and water or other problems caused purely by the circumstances of their birth, something none of us have any control over. The fact is you aren't going to help those people by being miserable yourself or by not accepting this Moment as being Perfect. Accepting the Perfection of Now is empowering and as such, makes you far more capable of doing something amazing to help others, should that be your chosen path. My approach to helping people that I encounter is to share resources I have beyond my needs, as well as trying to be an example of a content and happy individual in my interactions with those I meet.

Just like it's better to teach someone how to grow their own food than just give them a meal, I try and show people their own worth and equip them with the tools to be at Peace and experience Contentment, starting by recognising and identifying with, their true Self in the Here and Now as a starting point. Using simple meditation techniques over time will empower anyone to stay in the Moment longer and more frequently.

Remember, I was asked to work with one of the world's biggest pop groups; made a large amount of money - only to succumb to drug addiction and subsequently lose everything. Without the understanding I've been fortunate enough to gain through my experiences, I could easily be full of regrets and may even have decided to end my life. I had the World at my feet and my addiction prevented me from taking advantage of the opportunity. That's a big hit to overcome and if I hadn't been blessed with a deep seated understanding of Truth I may never have survived.

I learned that no amount of money or success can guarantee happiness, and that if you rely on anything outside your Self for your peace or contentment then you will be forever vulnerable as it can always be taken away. Worse still if you put conditions on your happiness that require certain things to happen, you're even more at risk of never finding peace and happiness. If for example you say "Well, if I had a bigger flat, then I'd be happy" all you're doing is making your happiness conditional on something you need to obtain.

Eckhart Tolle, author of the best-selling book The Power Of Now (which everyone should read!) said in the preface to his book; "People could sense that I was at peace and content and would ask me. "What is it you have, I want it!" My answer was "You already have it; your mind is just making too much noise for you to notice".

What did he mean by "too much noise"? He was talking about the constant train of thoughts that constantly course through your brain and which you identify with as being where your "I" resides, or the eye behind the person looking at the world out there. As I've said before these trains of thought tend to take you away from the Moment, either reliving the past or projecting into the future.

I appreciate you sticking with me as I share my experiences with you. I trust it has given you a clearer picture of the young man the band chose to work with back in late 1982. I know it may not be what you were expecting in a book about Duran Duran, but I felt it was important that you understood more about who I was as I started to work and live with the band. I hope that it will give some context to the rest of the book and how I saw the members of this incredible band that gave me the amazing opportunity.

Alex Sadkin

11
CRISIS, WHAT CRISIS?

A few days after the finished mix of Is There Something I Should Know? had been sent to EMI, I received an unwanted phone call from Michael Berrow. I was told that EMI had decided Alex Sadkin should produce the album and that my services were no longer required.

My fledgling career was in tatters. People would soon put two and two together and realise I had been out of my depth (which was not entirely true, not entirely untrue either). All the work I had put into co-producing the single would soon be forgotten, overshadowed by the skills Alex and Phil demonstrated in pulling the final mix together. It seemed I just wasn't good enough and might never recover from such a massive fall from grace.

I called the band, who were sympathetic, but ultimately knew they couldn't go against EMI and their managers, however much they may have felt for me at that stage. I pleaded with the Berrows but received even less sympathy, or frankly, interest.

Finally, I called Alex directly, told him what had happened and, to my amazement, he was shocked. He had not been told about the decision. Everyone just assumed he'd jump at the chance of being sole producer. The powers that be could not have misjudged his attitude more if they'd tried. "That's mad," he said. "As far as I can see, you're like a sixth member of the band."

He continued, "You understand the chemistry between them. You've already spent plenty of time with them which I haven't. It would be a folly to just get rid of all the work you've already put in getting to know how to work with them and understand them." He told me that he was going to tell EMI and the Berrows that he wouldn't take on the project without me.

Can you imagine my gratitude? His stance forced EMI and the Berrows to think again. I will never forget his attitude and, to be honest, generosity. Much of what he had said was undoubtedly true – I did understand the way the five members of the band worked together and could sense the chemistry between them. As the project moved forward, it did help me to resolve potential conflicts and help them perform to the best of their abilities. (Having said that, I never saw myself as being a sixth member of the band!)

Had Alex been a different kind of person, ambitious enough to tread on people in his way or wanting all the limelight for himself, he could quite easily have decided to be sole producer merely by taking no action, and I would have been off the team and reduced to starting from scratch, with battle scars. He had a real heart and a pure soul.

As our conversation continued, he elaborated. "You're a likeable guy and I've enjoyed seeing the way you work with the band. You've already established a meaningful rapport with each of them and they seem to enjoy having you around and working with you. Despite the problems you had mixing the single, the way the track was put together shows that you work well as a team player, and my sense is they trust your judgement. The problems with the mix were the result of you not monitoring the recording of the drums by the engineer. Had you done so you would have mixed it without any problems."

These were certainly reassuring words to hear from someone whose experience and track record commanded respect. He also suggested I learn more about the mechanics of how synthesisers worked, to have a better grasp of how to create interesting and impactful sounds, and that by doing so would also help improve my engineering skills, all of which would stand me in good stead as I moved forward.

I never found out directly how the band reacted to learning that a condition of Alex's involvement was that I was to remain part of the production team, but they seemed pleased enough to see me the next time we met up to start work on the writing of the material that would become Seven And The Ragged Tiger.

A major issue was resolved by my continued involvement, the elephant in the room that no one had considered when deciding to only use Alex to produce - which was that Duran Duran wanted their producer to help them write the songs. Alex was far too busy with other projects to take three months out of his schedule and be involved in the early phase of the album's development. It is not something producers are normally involved with as most bands write new songs all the time and have a catalogue of tunes to choose from for any upcoming recordings.

As I was free, I was more than happy to fill the role. It had several attractions for me, apart from the obvious fact of remaining part of the project. It gave me the chance to show the band that even after the mixing debacle, I had plenty to offer creatively. Even if I owed my ongoing presence to Alex, I was determined to justify their decision to work with me in the first place. I was looking forward to the opportunity to share some of the writing processes I had observed with Roxy Music and Alan Tarney. Although Simon and I had discussed some of these techniques during our time together in Sri Lanka, I'd only scratched the surface during the creation of the single.

French Chateau

12
WRITING & RECORDING WITH DURAN DURAN
SOUTH OF FRANCE
SPRING 1983

The band's accountants advised that because of their massive earnings from the first two albums, Duran Duran would benefit by taking a tax year. This meant that under the rules of the UK's tax system at the time, they would be free of a significant tax liability if they were only in the UK for a maximum of 30 days in the calendar year. Additionally, by not recording in the UK it meant they would not pay tax on UK sales, a significant saving for the poor struggling lads! The budget for the third album was in the region of £500,000 plus the cost of touring and marketing, which all meant that such a huge tax saving would make it easier for EMI to recoup their investment.

EMI and the Berrows had created a plan to rent a retreat at a large château in the south of France, where the band, girlfriends, managers (some of the time), and I could live in the height of rustic comfort and work on writing new songs.

We made our way to the south of France independently. I was driven from London by Michael Berrow in his Mercedes. To my delight, we stopped in Paris and spent a night in the world-famous George V hotel. It was my first taste of life in Five Star hotels. Despite this being just a regular single room, everything was done to make my stay as comfortable and luxurious as possible. Even the end of the loo roll was folded origami-style into some attractive pattern.

Being an ordinary guy from a modest background, I stuffed all the toiletries, hand towels and anything else not bolted down into my bags the next morning before we left. This was a good way to start my time in France and I wondered if our accommodation at the château would be of the same standard.

Michael's Mercedes was a gorgeous driving machine and the long journey south was painless as we cruised the well-organised French motorway system. Once we were near the château, just outside Cannes, navigation became a great deal harder with only paper maps. Eventually we saw the sign, half hidden in the bushes, adding to the adventure.

The beautifully appointed château was a splendour to behold, with its towered corners and palatially-styled arched main entrance. The rooms were perfectly proportioned, all boasting high ceilings with exposed dark timber supports. Having previously worked with a firm of architects, I relished the opportunity to explore the many features of this wonderful building and spent many a happy hour wandering around the place taking in the sumptuous details. My room, small and cosy, was up on the second or third floor, at the front of the building. I could look out from my window and see my place of work, the mobile recording truck, parked right below, in front of the main entrance. I didn't see much of the other guys' rooms. We all respected one another's privacy, since we were going to be spending just about every hour we were awake together, including luxurious meals.

The resident chef prepared three cooked meals for us every day. We would all convene, seated at a long, old-fashioned dining table easily big enough to seat the six of us, plus wives, girlfriends and managers. It was dining on a grand scale, breakfast, lunch and, le piece de la resistance, the evening meal. The standard of cuisine can best be compared to the quality of meals you'd expect at a first class, even a Michelin starred restaurant, and each meal was presented accordingly, although breakfast was an open buffet to allow for the various times each of us would rise and shine. We enjoyed mealtime.

Coming from a humble background, and more recently making do with what I could rustle up in an admittedly very fine kitchen at Gallery studio, I relished every meal – the food, the surroundings, and the good company. I was consciously storing away as many clear memories as I could, as though at any minute I'd wake up to find out it had all been a dream.

The main lounge room was huge and beautiful, reminding me of a way of living lost with the gathering pace of the era we now find ourselves in. I could imagine hunting parties gathering there before heading off for the ride through the glorious countryside that epitomizes that part of France. The lounge looked out over rough meadow rather than manicured lawns, to the edge of woods some 150 yards away, all part of the château's estate.

The enormous grounds and high surrounding trees kept us a well-guarded secret from anyone connected with the media, especially The Sun or other tabloid newspapers who were desperate for pictures of the band. A member of the paparazzi did manage to discover the location, and one of the band's security team found him hiding in the woods some distance away. With a long-range telescopic lens, he was able to see into the living room on the ground floor. Luckily the only member of the creative team he'd been able to see was me, which I don't think would have fetched much as a photo on the open market.

Following us to the château, an engineer from RAK Studios had driven their 24-track mobile recording truck down. It was parked outside the front of the building and the final part of the jigsaw was in place. The château had an attic space with pitched roof and wooden floor where the band set up, making a quirky but functional rehearsal space.

I used a variety of microphones, many of which were carried with us into the recordings done later at Air Studios in Montserrat, although as a full-blown studio they had a far wider selection. On Roger's kit I put a trusty AKG 414 inside the kick drum, combined with a sturdy Shure SM57 picking up the beater; an AKG C451 on top of the snare and another Shure SM57 underneath to pick up the rattles. To capture the ambience of the drum kit, I used four flat PZMs which today are a bit of a classic but were quite new then; two on the floor three metres in front of the kit, and another pair hung from the ceiling above the drums to capture the cymbals and a bit of additional room ambience.

I used a couple more SM57s for Roger and Andy's amps, plus direct line inputs from the back of each amp to give me more control over both instrument's sound and separation. Andy had an effects box that was inserted into the direct line input so he had complete control of the sound coming down to me in the truck. Lastly, most of Nick's synths were fed into monitors so they could all hear them, and they were hardwired straight into the desk in the mobile.

With Simon using yet another SM57 for his vocals and a couple of others on stands for when any of the guys wanted to chip in with backing vocals, or even if they had suggestions for melody lines for Simon, we were set. There was a small 14 channel mixer in the attic which took a few attempts to get a decent headphone mix for everyone, searching for the right balance between live drums and Andy and John's baffled, screened off amps.

Mobile recording truck

Public domain

When playing any electronic instrument plugged into an amp and loudspeaker, you have two ways of hearing it. One way is to place a microphone in front of the amplifier's speaker and create a feed that can be sent to a recording desk and on to a tape recorder, or to a huge public address system that creates a huge sound capable of filling vast venues such as Wembley Arena. The other way you can hear any electronic instrument is by plugging it directly into a mixing desk and then on to a tape recorder. Each of the two methods has its own sound and benefits. The amplifier can be heard by the musician directly if they're in the same room, whereas they can't hear an electronic feed going straight into the mixer. However, for the engineer trying to record the instrument's sound, the option of feeding directly into the mixing desk is clean, lacks any ambient sound, and as such is far easier to control.

Usually, especially in a concert, when the engineer wants to create a live sound, they will use a mixture of the two feeds; one from the microphone in front of the artist's amplifier and the other the direct feed into the mixing desk. In France, having these two sound sources for Andy's guitar, John's bass and Nick's synths allowed me to mix the live sound and the line feed to create the most controlled sound possible. It gave me the control I needed to record each part cleanly, which was essential when you consider how much ambience is created by the volume Duran Duran played at, especially in an untreated room not designed for playing loud live music. To complete the picture, I needed to incorporate some of Simon's vocals and any potential backing vocals from the others. It wasn't easy to find a balance that suited everyone's needs but we managed it in the end.

Down at ground level, I sat in the relatively confined environment of the RAK mobile truck outdoors. Equipped with a small API console, a very compact mixing desk well suited to mobile recording use and a 3M 24-track recorder, which I ran at 15 inches per second (ips) to get 40 minutes out of each reel of tape as opposed to the normal 20 minutes you'd get running at 30ips. With the slower tape speed, you lose a bit of quality, but we were still very much at the ideas stage and didn't anticipate using the material recorded for anything other than demos. With an eye not only on economy, but also the lack of space to store dozens of bulky reels of tape in the truck, audio quality was secondary to such practicalities in this instance.

I would sit and listen to the guys messing about up top and whenever I heard anything I thought interesting or worthwhile, I'd make a note of the time showing on the tape counter, and if something really caught my attention I'd actually call upstairs and tell them to come down and listen back to what I felt might be the kernel of a song. By recording everything the guys played, it meant being able to take advantage of any moments of inspiration, be it a great groove, an emotive chord progression, a hooky bass line, or a compelling guitar riff.

I felt the one with the hardest role at this stage was probably Simon as he really needed some music to work with, unless he either wrote lyrics before there was any music (as a poet might), or developed melody lines that the other guys would develop a chord progression around. So sometimes he sat out the jam sessions. Simon not always being in the room with the other four had its advantages. Firstly, he would hear things fresh, often enabling a more objective take on any new ideas. It also meant he physically didn't become jaded which I feared was a risk if he was sitting around with nothing much to work with in the early stages. He was on hand when called upon to write words to a set of chords, a groove, or sometimes something that was closer to being a completed song. I helped the guys explore the various song writing methods I'd learned from Bryan Ferry and Alan Tarney, as well as some ideas of my own that I'd developed as a non-musician during the recording of the New Asia tracks.

All in all, it was a perfect place to act as our base camp, and hopefully inspire plenty of creativity. Despite the many and varied attractions, such as fast cars (including a particularly nice 5 Series BMW), trail bikes, and the location itself, we knuckled down and formed a plan of attack. We soon developed a routine, centred around the band coming up with ideas for new songs. Sometimes I'd have to crack the whip, but everyone worked hard, aware of the pressure we were under.

One thing I'd learned during my time at Gallery was that there are as many ways of writing songs as there are songs! This was one of the lessons I'd hoped to impart to Duran Duran, that working the way they did, not writing until they needed something to record, they really needed to optimise their process and not let any potential gems slip through their fingers. The first successful approach I'd encountered that really achieved that was the method used by Bryan Ferry that I described in the earlier chapter about the making of Avalon and Jealous Guy. In essence, Bryan would play simple chord progressions that producer Rhett Davies or I would record onto cassettes and notate each section so at a later date we could experiment by combining (say) progression 5 with number 32 and see if the transition between them worked and could be the start of a song, a technique that capitalised on every drop of inspiration that came along.

Another weapon in our arsenal of tools at the château was a programmable drum machine. With this device, on the rare occasions where it seemed appropriate, I could put a beat together, send it up to Roger's headphones, and he could start bouncing ideas around the theme I'd given him.

With the band ensconced in the attic and me sitting in the RAK mobile, 24-track tape rolling, the Duran Duran song idea factory gradually started to come to life. Jamming at first, and then with input from me and their own judgement about what they were coming up with, the seeds of songs started to develop.

The tracks that were to become the three big singles were created quite early in proceedings – Union Of The Snake, New Moon On Monday, and The Reflex. They were quickly etched into our collective memories as they were clearly commercial tracks. That doesn't mean the rest of the album had any less love poured into it. To me, a well-balanced album has tracks that strike you immediately. Typically those tend to be the singles, whereas others are growers (deep cuts) and take time to appreciate more. Radio and MTV producers didn't have time for their listeners to discover these hidden gems, so songs that grabbed the attention on the first listen were usually picked as singles.

In those days, we made albums intended to be listened to from beginning to end rather than the single-track streaming and download culture we have now. Apart from rare exceptions such as legacy acts with a built-in fanbase, most artists and their labels focus far more on individual tracks today, and albums are an afterthought at worst, or a collection of singles at best.

One of the most memorable moments from that period is the creation of Union Of The Snake. It showed up during a low point when everybody seemed to have temporarily run out of fresh ideas. I decided to experiment, using the Linn drum machine as a starting point. I thought Roger might welcome some fresh rhythmic input so I started to program.

This was soon after David Bowie had released Let's Dance, his biggest single and biggest album to date. We loved the track, so I decided to delve into the depths of its drum pattern and attempt to duplicate the infectious groove. I discovered with some amazement that unlike most bass drum patterns that repeat after either one, two or sometimes four bars, Let's Dance took eight bars to come back round to its start again. It was genius, really, I was so impressed and excited at this unexpected discovery. I put something together with this in mind and called up to the guys and told them to come and listen to what I'd come up with.

Roger and the rest of the band set about learning the pattern. Roger nailed it, John started a trademark bass line and within a couple of sessions the bulk of Union Of The Snake was completed, one of those songs that almost seems to write itself, ideas coming effortlessly, musical parts flowing. All the while, Simon wandered around trying out ideas in his head or under his breath. Slowly but surely, he'd come up with the lyrics and melody lines, in no particular order that I could discern from listening to him.

We usually found ways to keep ourselves amused during lapses in creativity or necessary R&R. At one point Michael Berrow arrived with a brand-new grey Ferrari that he bought in Switzerland and drove back to our base to be greeted by plenty of raised eyebrows. At about the same time, I think it was John who turned up in an equally pristine but less prestigious VW Golf GTI. The enormous difference in cost of the two vehicles created the first seeds of discontent that would eventually lead to conversations about the nature of the deal the Berrows had created for themselves.

Another telling incident that occurred during our time at the château was when the Berrows went missing for several weeks. No one seemed to know where they'd gone. Calls to various people failed to produce any leads. It transpired that they were flying, mainly by helicopter and at great expense, around South America, supposedly scouting possible locations for a Duran Duran feature film that no one (including the band) had any knowledge of. The whole thing reeked of an exotic vacation on the band's dime.

The advice given to those involved in great heists is always the same: lie low in the initial period immediately after the scam. Do not start splashing the cash. Many would-be career criminals, impatient to start enjoying the fruits of their labour, have tripped on this most basic of hurdles, and the Berrows were clearly not immune. Since the only way they were coming into such large amounts of the folding stuff was through the proceeds of their protégés, it wasn't long before the band started to think about the nature of their deal with the Berrows and how fair it was.

Along with these relatively moderate levels of extra-curricular activities, the ongoing process of song creation was still progressing. In the evenings, I would spend time with each of the guys, getting to know them better as individuals, forming opinions as to their interests, what made them excited and what left them cold. I saw this as being an essential part of gaining a more rounded appreciation of the chemistry between the five members of the band.

To take a slight detour, I have a confession to make. Before I started to work with Duran Duran, they were nowhere near being my favourite band. I was into much less pop material, preferring more left field, art music. Without having given the issue much thought, I had bought into the widely held belief that they were a manufactured

band, produced according to some great Svengali's vision. Once I started to work with them on that first single those impressions were dispatched quickly. If memory serves, when we started work on recording the album in Montserrat, we worked for around six weeks solid without taking a break. This was not in any way, shape or form a puppet band. After first witnessing their professionalism at Good Earth during the making of the single it was reinforced by them showing the same values during this writing period in southern France.

At the château work proceeded if not at a breakneck pace then certainly consistently. One of my great EVAs (Extra Vehicular Activities) was to take charge of the communal BMW 5 Series. I had something of a history in motorsport, kart racing when I was about 12 and even a few races in a rather uncompetitive Formula Ford single seater. It was why, before my art teacher (and old friend of David Bowie) Robin Gray was shocked to discover that rather than going to university to study fine art, I had enrolled for an apprenticeship with Porsche UK. I would proceed to thrash the BMW to within an inch of its life (and often mine) roaring around the curling roads of rural France. I had a few close shaves, one where I looked in my rear-view mirror to see the back of a truck sticking out from the side of the road. It was a close shave but looked like no harm had been done and although I didn't go back to make totally sure as I should have done with hindsight, I did wait to see the driver's door swing open, saw him step down and walk around his truck.

Such exertions helped relieve the sometimes monotonous confines of my small working office in the RAK mobile truck. It was only ever intended for recording live gigs where you'd park round the back of a venue in the morning, mic everything up, record the show, then send the master tapes away to be mixed elsewhere. To use it for three months pushed its comfort levels to the max. I often found myself looking for ways of keeping myself amused, all the time listening for any nugget coming from upstairs as the band played away. They had good days and bad days, just like any other set of musicians working through the creative process.

What did start to concern me was the calendar stuck inside one of the truck's front windows which showed how much time remained before we'd be expected back in London with an album's worth of songs written. The first time this struck me, we were barely halfway towards our target of ten songs (ideally plus a couple of spares too), but with over half of our time gone. I felt my first pangs of concern. What to do, approach the guys and point out how much time we had left, or would that prove counterproductive? On the other hand, they surely needed to be made aware of how rapidly time was passing, and that we were falling behind schedule.

I wrestled with the dilemma for the rest of the afternoon before deciding I had no choice but to confront them all about the situation and face their reaction, whatever it may be. I suggested we take stock of what we had so far and decide what ideas were any good, which were well developed, and which could be knocked into shape with some hard work and clever tactics. Thinking back on that period, as our stay in France drew to a close, I think it was the first time I'd felt the need to assert myself as their producer.

Their reaction to my delivering the bad news was mixed. The two who took the facts onboard most acutely were Andy and Nick. Which is not to say Simon, John or Roger were any less concerned, but I sensed they looked to the other two to sort it out, to make things right. In that respect there really was a marked difference between Nick and Andy and the others. The two of them had a real maturity, they already had a clear awareness of the implications of the album not being good enough, something that still seemed a long way off to the others.

Unbeknownst to the band, I'd been making lists of sections they'd played, that I felt had the potential to be added to other parts to create something resembling a song. I suggested I spend more time in the attic, as I could respond more quickly and a bit more intuitively to what they were doing if I was actually in the room. There were no egos involved, we all wanted to put together the best songs possible in the time we had left. I could leave the 24-track rolling, set a stopwatch, and run down roughly every 40 minutes to change the tape.

Finally, I would spend my evenings going through all the recordings we'd done that day looking for any little gems that had been overlooked at the time and see if there was anything worth revisiting. We felt we had a good plan in place to use the remaining few weeks at our disposal to best effect and set about putting those ideas into action. Obvious strong contenders like Union Of The Snake, The Reflex and New Moon On Monday were all pretty much done and dusted in terms of their overall shapes and chord progressions. So now we needed another seven or eight songs and we'd have the guts of the album done. There was light at the end of the tunnel, but still plenty left to do.

It was an amazing way to write an album, all in a lengthy session where we were, in effect, living in the studio. The fact that we got as much done as we did was testament to the work the band and I put in during those months. Writing songs is about timing, and having enough time to experiment and grow. The Berrow brothers were probably wrong to think that a couple of months was enough time for the band to come up with 11 or 12 songs. With time a finite and non-renewable resource, we were somewhat in the hands of fate as to whether inspiration came or not. Making music, like any creative process, is not a predictable process; writing songs is not an automated production line like building cars.

As well as cataloguing existing sections, I looked for other possible starting points for new material, like a drum groove or bass riff played by Roger or John to try and create something from which Nick and Andy might find inspiration. It can be so close yet so far in these situations. You know that a solid guitar riff played atop an equally solid beat could be all that it takes for Nick to then come up with a Ferry-esque moody pad and a chord progression that could evolve into another new song. We tried anything and everything.

Being in France at that time coincided with the itinerary of David Bowie's Serious Moonlight tour, promoting the Let's Dance album. The Duran Duran entourage were all issued with AAA passes for the concert at a 12,000-capacity outdoor amphitheatre in Fréjus that had previously hosted acts such as Rod Stewart, Queen and Iron Maiden, a breath-taking venue for a live performance. Bowie, buoyed by the huge success of the single and album, ruled the stage as a titan at the top of his game. Being able to witness proceedings from every vantage point, as I had with Supertramp, gave me a unique insight into the sheer quality of the band and production Bowie had at his disposal. They were so on it, exuded such huge confidence and panache. It was a genuine treat to behold. After numerous encores, as much as I wanted to act the fan and go backstage afterwards to talk to the many legendary members of this band - as well as the main man himself of course - the pressures of being with Duran Duran meant we had to leave almost before the final curtain fell. As it happened, I wouldn't have long to wait for an unexpected opportunity to talk to Bowie at length.

Amongst other stars using the sand, sea and sun of Cannes as a backdrop was Elton John, who was there to shoot the video for his new single, I'm Still Standing, with gifted Australian director Russell Mulcahy, who had also directed some of Duran Duran's most iconic videos to date. After the choreography and various close-ups were in the can, Elton took over one of the top hotels on the seafront where he hosted a post-shoot shindig, attended by the rich and famous. Once again, my association with the band gained me entry to this exclusive gathering. And I lapped it up. I loved brushing shoulders with the cream of the crop of 1980s pop and rock royalty. I spotted Bowie and made a beeline towards him. What people don't always realise is that prior to the release of Space Oddity, Bowie, still wearing his hair long and sporting baggy trousers, founded a new wave folk club called The Beckenham Arts Lab with my high school arts teacher Robin Gray, who would take me and a couple of school chums to these events.

I was now relatively used to rubbing shoulders with pop stars but as when I first met Bryan Ferry, meeting David Bowie was something special as he had played such a major part throughout my formative years. How different I would have been without his music is impossible to say, but you all know that when a band or artist becomes an obsession at a certain age, it tends to stay with you for life!

So I was somewhat nervous, despite being in such exalted company, to walk up and introduce myself to the great man. Sadly it's not always the case, but in this instance I wasn't disappointed by the experience. Bowie was as friendly as could be and once we hit on the common ground of the Beckenham Arts Lab and Robin Gray, we were just a couple of buddies talking about the old times. I naturally told him about how much his albums meant to me, much as I had when talking to Phil Manzanera about Roxy Music, although I didn't monopolise Bowie for three hours! I reminded Bowie of these early days of his career, and to my relief not only did he remember them but with a fondness that seemed to bring on a pang of nostalgia. He had happy memories of those avant-garde evenings, and we shared an enjoyable period of reflection, full of positive memories combined with a bit of 'look at us now' back slapping. With his passing in January 2016, I thank the gods I had that chance to meet and talk to one of the most important artists of my teenage years, maybe of the twentieth century. I know people often say how ordinary stars are when you meet them, or how they can come away disappointed at how frosty their idol was. Not me. Not with Bowie.

Later that same evening, the band and I explored the nightlife of Cannes with Nile Rodgers and Bernard Edwards of Chic for an unusual and unforgettable evening, especially one awkward moment where the whole of our party snaked our way through to the back of a night club, only to realise it was completely full of gay men. No problem with that, but not what we had in mind, so we turned on our heels to retrace our steps as quickly and furtively as possible.

A much bigger issue was the attitude Nile and Bernard adopted towards me. I soon realised that I was viewed by the ambitious pair as being someone that essentially was standing in their way. They obviously wanted to work with Duran Duran so their attitude was to totally ignore me, despite my attempts to engage in conversation, and unashamedly attempt to sell their own credentials to the band. It was a sadly distasteful example of the cutthroat nature of the music industry, which, sequestered at Gallery and then in the RAK mobile, I hadn't really experienced. It was a rude awakening to a naïve newcomer about the darker side of the business elements of music, especially in contrast to the selfless kindness and comradeship Alex Sadkin had demonstrated in keeping me involved in the Duran Duran album at all costs.

I am the first to acknowledge Nile and Bernard's undoubted musical talents, which border on genius. There's certainly no denying their positive impact on the history of pop music. Nonetheless, the ploys they used to belittle me and even to a lesser extent Alex's contribution were shallow, leaving a bad taste in the mouth that has never really left me unfortunately.

Having said all that, Nile was a man possessed and would go on to produce hit after hit, having already created a style of guitar playing that helped define disco and funk music, a style often copied, never bettered. I'm sure if Nile ever reads this, he won't remember how they treated me, or even remember me amongst all the other partying and all the fun. But it was a bit of a wakeup call for me. I'd heard scuttlebutt that on my being chosen to produce Is There Something I Should Know? managers of better-known producers had made concerned troll calls to both EMI and Tritec, the Berrows' company, questioning the wisdom of using this unknown upstart rather than their personal charge.

So, I should have been more aware of the feathers that had been ruffled by my appointment long before it manifested that night in Cannes. Ultimately, I guess it was a draw – Nile remixed The Reflex single, and I'm credited with co-producing the album and singles.

Back at the château as the day approached when the RAK mobile truck was due to start its long drive back to London, it was all hands to the pumps while we looked for that elusive spark of inspiration that would help create one more track for the album. Apart from the three singles, the rest of the album was far from complete. We realised the band had not been given enough time to write the number of songs required, but we were going to have to deal with it. Although I wasn't involved, I can only imagine that ahead of the creation of their first two albums, they had built up a wealth of ideas and so turning them into songs was a relatively straightforward process.

It's hard to remember which of the remaining songs eventually used on the album had their gestation in France and which ones evolved later. I've read a lot over the years about a demo that was supposedly recorded when we were in France that was originally called The Seventh Stranger but went on to be given the album's title Seven And The Ragged Tiger which was never used. Confused yet? I am! I've even had people send me terrible sounding sub-bootleg quality recordings that must have been a cassette taken off the tapes from the mobile truck. Maybe a sharp tape op at RAK thought they could make a few quid putting out Duran Duran bootlegs, thankfully apart from this one piece of garbage I've not heard any others so hopefully they've all been wiped long ago! Apparently, this demo went on to evolve into a song that gave the album its name. As you know The Seventh Stranger is the final track on the original album. As for this other song or demo, I don't remember a different song coming out of the ideas that made up The Seventh Stranger.

We ended our time in France with plenty of recordings jamming in the attic, mixed down from the 24-track tape onto ¼" stereo. From that we ran off enough cassettes for each of us to have one, and some spares for Alex Sadkin and a few people at EMI including A&R chief Dave Ambrose who'd first signed the band. Although the guys hadn't managed to write enough complete songs for the album, we hoped we at least had enough material and ideas to stand us in good stead for the next stage of its evolution.

Aerial view of Air Studios Montserrat

13
MAIN ALBUM RECORDING AT AIR STUDIOS
MONTSERRAT
SUMMER 1983

Bands and songs came and went through the singles chart but apart from those already established in 1982 like Culture Club and Spandau Ballet, there were no new contenders in the space occupied by Duran Duran. Following Is There Something I Should Know? entering the chart at number one, the band had re-established their position as the top teen band. The Blitz club nights at Camden's Electric Ballroom, a favourite haunt of Boy George and other members of the New Romantics, heralded the next iteration of the movement. This saw the birth of a tougher, more eclectic sound with bands like Depeche Mode experimenting with early samplers on their ground-breaking albums Construction Time Again and Some Great Reward; and expert producers such as Trevor Horn working with bands like Frankie Goes To Hollywood (alongside Propaganda bringing in a harder, purer electronic sound).

We didn't have that many studios to choose from, owing to the band taking their tax year outside the UK. In addition, there was a reason why we couldn't go to the United States, I seem to recall it was a union issue as we wanted to use at least three session musicians from the States. Consequently, if we decided to escape Europe, it came down to a choice between Compass Point in the Bahamas or Air (actually an acronym, short for Associated Independent Recording) on the island of Montserrat, set up by Beatles producer George Martin. We chose the latter as it had closer ties with EMI and at that time, Compass Point was just losing out to Montserrat in the coolest-studio-to-go-to stakes. There was no technical difference between the two facilities particularly, although our start at Montserrat in the end was far from convincing!

Before moving to Montserrat, it was decided that after the almost continuous work during our time in France, we would take a short four-day break in New York. We landed at JFK, and after the drive into Manhattan, checked in at a Holiday Inn. At that time, the wider American public did not really know who Duran Duran were, so we were able to go out to restaurants and move around quite freely, even if in limousines. (The next time we were in the Big Apple for the 1984 tour, we couldn't even go down to the lobby, not even little old me!)

The Holiday Inn was a perfectly decent hotel but struck me as being somewhat generic, with nothing special about it at all. If we were to properly enjoy our short time in New York, I felt we needed more lavish surroundings. I picked up the phone, asked to be put through to Nick and enquired what he thought of our accommodation. Not much, was his reply, to which I agreed. I suggested we sought out more salubrious surroundings. As we mulled over the hotels we knew about in New York, Nick asked me where Bryan Ferry stayed. That I knew – the Carlyle. Well if it was good enough for our Bryan, we figured it'd be pretty darn good for us. We next sought to enlist the rest of the band, but the only other member that could be bothered to make a move was Andy. So, Nick, Andy and I went down to the lobby and into the street where there was a limo at our disposal 24/7. I instructed the driver to take us to the Carlyle.

Once we arrived, we were stunned to be told that the hotel did not encourage or even want pop stars staying there. We were informed that most of those people staying were residents, millionaire's widows (usually with a clutch of annoying toy dogs in tow), and that the hotel avoided the kind of attention celebrities attracted. We assured the desk clerk we weren't going to be attracting hordes of fans but they remained unconvinced. We would have to discuss the matter with the hotel manager. Duran Duran were not used to having people say no to them, certainly not at hotel reception desks.

We were invited to sit by a prim, slightly uptight and incredibly camp individual who proceeded to try and convince us we'd be much happier at various other establishments. However, with the knowledge now firmly implanted in Nick and Andy's minds that this was where Ferry stayed, they were determined that we were staying here too, and made that clear to the manager. With reluctant acceptance, he seemed genuinely stumped as to what to do. Then, sensing triumph (prematurely, as it turned out), he realised that even though they would after all be happy to accommodate us, the only room available was a suite on the twenty-eighth floor, in the region of $5,000 a night ($13,000 in 2021). In an instant, Andy stood up, held out his hand and said, "We'll take it!" The manager, totally taken aback, nervously shook Andy's hand, then Nick's and finally mine as the three of us grinned at him like naughty boys who'd just been given the keys to the toy shop. The deflated manager proceeded to show us out of his office, back to the front desk, where we went through signing in as we handed over our passports. He collected the relevant keys and led us to a distinct pair of lifts that only went to the top three or four floors, including our suite.

At this height in the building's layout, there were only two suites per floor. This meant we had views out of three sides of the skyscraper, located on 35 East 76th Street, a couple of blocks from Central Park. It was the height of luxury for the 1980s. Today it would likely seem a bit downmarket compared to some of the seven-star hotels around, especially in Asia and the Middle East. But to us, or anyone back in 1983, this was it!

The suite was huge. Apart from at least three bedrooms, there was a lounge, a kitchen, dining room, several bathrooms, and a seemingly endless number of bathrooms, as Americans call toilets. All the furnishings and fabrics were of the finest quality. It was obvious the manager was scared rigid that we were going to trash the place. As he showed us around, he constantly pointed out just how pale and easily stained the variously patterned fabrics were. Compared to my first trip to New York when I was sent by Situation Two to promote New Asia, this was quite a change. During that week-long trip, I had slept on the floor of an apartment rented by a friend of my label boss. Over the next four days we lived like kings, so much so that my room service bill alone was in the thousands. Don't ask.

Another first during our stay at the Carlyle was when Nick and Andy came to me to express concerns they had about the terms of the band's deal with the Berrow brothers. I was older than the band's eldest member (Simon) but younger than the Berrows, which gave me an ideal position to act as confidante to the band. They expressed their suspicions that in fact the deal between them and their managers was not quite fair. Obviously, without having the actual contracts to look at all I could do was listen to what they thought the deal was. After hearing the details they outlined to me, the only help I felt was fair for me to give was to advise them to seek professional advice at the earliest opportunity. This they did and a while later they split with Tritec. I think that says all you need to know about the terms of the deal they had!

I was woken after our first night in residence by the wails of a maid who, upon entering the suite around noon, found the aftermath of the previous night's partying, with various non-residents sprawled on sofas and on the floor, as well as in every bedroom. "Oh my Lord, oh my Lord!" she screamed in total disgust. We hadn't done any permanent damage but the pristine suite we'd moved into the day before now looked, to say the least, a little lived in.

As a strange coincidence my oldest of friends, someone I've known since I was eleven, happened to be in New York at the same time. After checking it was OK with Nick and Andy, I contacted Neil and invited him to come and stay with us for a few days. Neil was on a short, low-budget trip, his first stay in New York, so for me to be able to offer him the sumptuous luxury of the top floor of The Carlyle was quite a buzz. Rather than doing a whole heap of tourist stuff, I think we spent most of the two or three days he stayed with us using room service, running up huge tabs and indulging in everything the suite had to offer. I realised that from our perch in the heavens I could see a branch of Tower Records and I remember saying, "Every time someone goes in there and buys a Duran Duran record, we're all making a few cents. God bless America!"

We had a limo on call as I mentioned and were able to come and go as we pleased. We went to some of the finest restaurants in Greenwich Village and did a bit of wandering around, but generally we were there to build up our energy for the next stretch of the album. One expedition we did go on was when Andy came to me and wanted to see if our limo driver could get some weed. Unsurprisingly he said he could but at a price. Andy handed over $300 and we sat back in our long black limo as our driver headed downtown. As the streets became full of potholes, darker, and narrower, our driver turned around and said, "Better hit them door locks brother, we's looking a mite conspicuous, if you get me." We got him. He pulled up, wound down his window, handed over some cash and we were away. When I lived in New York many years later, I found out that what we'd actually paid for was $30 worth, not a bad mark-up for our friend the driver. At least we were happy with the weed, and indeed made one more such trip downtown.

We had a relaxing last couple of days then it was time for us to head off on the next stage of our adventure, the flight to Montserrat, as work on the recording of the album beckoned. All too soon, we were being transported by limousine to the airport for the two-hour flight to Miami, where we transferred to a small twin prop plane that would take us on the short flight across the ocean to the volcanic island of Montserrat.

The reason such a small plane had to be used was due to the restrictions of the demanding approach and short runway of Montserrat's W. H. Bramble Airport (also known as Blackburne), today locked inside the volcanic exclusion zone and replaced in 2005 by John A. Osborne airport in the north of the island. It's not a flight I'd recommend to anyone with even a mild fear of flying. Our approach was breath-taking as our small bird dropped from an impossibly steep angle. But as this book and Duran Duran's continued presence suggests, we made it safely down and taxied across the grass to the small parking area. Less terra, more firma as Nile Rodgers is fond of saying these days! We had a spectrum of views of the flight out to the remote island. To me the journey was quite an adventure. In planes that small, every squall of turbulence gives the impression that the plane is about to shake itself apart.

Our plan to relocate to the West Indies and Air's luxury residential studio was realised. We'd arrived safe and in one piece. Not only that, but miraculously, all our luggage and equipment also made it intact.

Once on the ground, things became 'island style', with everything moving at a leisurely pace. You walked, carrying your luggage, or maybe had the use of a modest wheel cart that was pushed and pulled across the grass to the immigration, arrivals and departures building (a small shed). The process of becoming a temporary resident of this charming island was simplicity itself. I'm not sure how you'd be treated if you arrived as a regular tourist, but since the only real reason to come there was Air, I don't actually think there were anything but hotels for visiting relatives of the inhabitants, rather than for tourists. Although anyone could visit the island, its black sand beaches and sulphurous smell must have meant there were not many casual visitors. Perhaps there were also scientific studies being done on a regular basis as it was an active volcano (this became all too apparent a decade or so later).

By this time, Alex Sadkin's workload had eased up and he was finally able to join us. The start of recording proper could begin. We'd all worked with Alex when mixing Is There Something I Should Know? at RAK Studio in London so there were no introductions required. I think he joined us at JFK, so made the flight to Miami and then onto Montserrat with the rest of us. The studio manager was at the airport to meet us all and drive us up to the studio, which sat on top of one of the island's peaks.

Air Studios Montserrat Control Room with Sir George Martin © Martyn Goddard

Montserrat was created over many millions of years by eruptions from a volcano called La Soufrière, which erupted with devastating effect in July 1995, six years after the studio itself had been destroyed by Hurricane Hugo in September 1989 (just after The Rolling Stones had recorded Steel Wheels at Air). Although it could have been repaired, the constant threat of such future disasters meant that to do so made little business sense to George Martin. Over the decade that it existed, more than 70 albums were made there, including Ghost In The Machine and Synchronicity by The Police, Brothers In Arms by Dire Straits, and Power Windows and Hold Your Fire by Rush. Many more legendary artists recorded there including Paul McCartney, Stevie Wonder, and Eric Clapton, so it was a great loss when it was destroyed. It seemed that great bands went in and great albums came out! It was to be our home and base for about eight weeks in total.

After settling into our comfortable accommodation and enjoying the first of many beautifully prepared meals, we had a group meeting to assess the situation we were facing. The first to express concern was Alex. He had expected us to arrive there with the whole album written and ready to start recording. I had explained to Alex how the band wrote from scratch when the two of us were fixing the mix on Is There Something I Should Know? - but I didn't go into detail and he was too involved with what he was doing at the time to have taken it fully onboard. I don't think he really understood that when we arrived in France we started with nothing, and that I wondered if enough time had been allocated for this part of making the album. He shared my concerns but we agreed, "It is what it is, we'll crack on and make the best album we can." Understanding how the lads worked put into context our apparent lack of progress. Although it now made sense to him, it didn't alter the fact that we had an awful lot to do and were immediately under pressure. We took stock of the work that lay ahead, and the fact that if we were to make the proposed pre-Christmas 1983 release, we needed to really crack on.

Having catalogued the music and ideas we had created in France, we knew how much writing still needed to be done to have enough material to fill an album. In the days when vinyl was by far the dominant medium, album lengths varied from as short as 30 minutes up to a physical limit of around 45 minutes, as one side of a vinyl LP could only comfortably hold about 22 minutes of music. Above that, to fit the grooves on, sacrifices had to be made in terms of volume and audio quality. Our aim was around 40 minutes (final duration is 37:36).

People took various approaches to this time restriction. Some preferred to start proceedings with a big track that grabbed the listener's interest right from the moment the album started, then took a step down in intensity before gradually growing to end the side on a high. Then the second side would typically follow a similar path but with a less intense opening, a sustained couple of tracks in the middle with possibly the best track of all to end side two. Obviously, the material you had at your disposal influenced the approach you adopted. In our position, with a certain number of songs still needing to be penned, we lacked the luxury of being able to position the tracks we already had and then know what types of songs we needed to fill in the gaps.

We decided to start by recording the songs that were written or close to being written, and then look at building the unfinished songs. Even those tracks that were considered finished still needed to be recorded from scratch, as the versions captured in France were demos, particularly since we'd elected to record at 15ips which meant lower audio quality.

One of the first things we considered was the session musicians we'd like to bring in. There were several top-class musicians that both Alex and I had worked with, but in the end I deferred to his greater experience, relying on his choices of who to call upon for the additional talents we needed. One person Alex knew, who I had heard of but never worked with, was percussionist Raphael DeJesus. I'm starting with Raphael because of all the people we used during our time at Montserrat, he was the one whose skills struck me as being irreplaceable. Something about this guy just had me mesmerised every time he went into the live room to record a part. His favourite instruments were a collection of shakers, made from different sized containers filled with various types of dried beans, pulses and split peas. He had rubber wrists and by flexing them he could create shaker sounds of varying pitches and speeds, bathing every track in a groove lubricant, oiling the beats, making them hang together. It's amazing, on reflection, how such a simple thing as a shaker can be so powerful. What might otherwise have seemed a slightly stiff groove would suddenly flow perfectly. Watching and listening to him at work was one of the highlights of my time spent in recording studios.

Like all professional session musicians, he had a full kit of instruments and we used plenty of them. His percussion instruments produced sounds that created a feature in a track and we used some of these to create an accent or add a percussive pattern (as an example I really like the wood block on Shadows On Your Side), but invariably it was the shakers that we returned to time and time again.

We brought in two of the best backing vocalists around at the time, Michelle Cobbs and BJ Nelson, two girls from New York that Alex had worked with previously and who could do anything you needed on a track. Perfect pitch combined with oodles of emotion meant the parts they added were luxuriant. Their performances created a certain sheen, which made one of the first things I asked them to do even more unexpected.

We were working on The Reflex and for some reason the idea occurred to me that what we needed for the bridge was the sound of kids singing in a playground. I told them to just do a kind of "la la la la" in time and tune with the section. Funnily enough, when Nile Rodgers came to remix the track for its single release, he chose to use their backing vocals to start the track. Strange how things turn out. You can hear the girls' voices on many of the tracks, sometimes as enhancements of Simon's vocal melody lines, on others as a texture, or subtle harmonic tone sitting under the other vocal parts in the track. In whatever capacity we used Michelle and BJ, their talents shone through – precise, pitch perfect, full of character.

Alex didn't lord it over me, never thwarted my creativity or my input one little bit, but I relied on him to make sure that everything was being done to the right technical standards. For instance, when we started on The Reflex and adopted the drum pattern from the demo, I knew the part much more intimately than Alex. I therefore told him what the groove was about, what I felt we needed to do with the bass drum, the snare and the hi-hat, and how I heard the groove working – when you're producing a drummer, you've got to relate to what he's doing with each of his limbs, because the groove depends on how he interweaves the various elements. I conveyed that to Alex, who was quick on the uptake, and he then took charge of getting the right sounds. Since I was usually on the band's side of the fence, making all of them more aware of the rhythmic quality of their performances, he provided us with a perfectly balanced production approach.

We decided to bring an engineer from RAK in London, Peter Wade-Schwier, whom both Alex and I had worked with and had full confidence in. Montserrat had assistant engineers who knew where everything was; how things like the patch bay on the mixing desk worked; what channel on the desk each socket in the live room came in on, and beyond such necessary knowledge they were probably good enough to have engineered at other facilities. However, as just about every act that went to the island brought their own engineer, it made little sense for Air to pay the kind of money a top flight engineer was earning at that time, anything up to £900 a day for the very best people.

As it was the most complete song written and one of the strongest tracks, we started off recording The Reflex. If there was something irreplaceable on the two-inch tapes that we had used in France for any song, we'd build up the new tracks on there. However, The Reflex was started from scratch in Montserrat because it was a song that needed excellent technical quality and really sharp drum sounds. Neither Alex nor I had to do very much as Roger and John put their parts down. There was the odd mistake of course which was easily repaired by starting recording at the point where the error occurred and using a technique called dropping in.

This was common practice in multi-track recording to tape. You would record the part from start to end of a track. Then on listening back to what was a perfectly good take you might find a fluffed note. So, rather than replacing the whole take, you would line up the tape a few bars ahead of where the mistake occurred. The musician would then play along with his recorded part and at the point where the mistake was, the engineer would hit the record button and overwrite the old mistake with the newly played, hopefully correct part, thus dropping in – and then dropping back out again. If the bulk of a take was good, it was far quicker to drop in and correct mistakes even if there were several points at which it was necessary to do so. It could be a challenge if there was something great on the original take just before or just after the mistake. "Can we get in there?" became the question. And just as importantly, "Can we get out?" The skills of a good engineer in the analogue age included sharp physical reflexes when faced with such a challenge, drop in BAM! capture the corrected note and BAM! out of record mode again. We did it!

Before long, we had the solid rhythm section down and were ready to move on. We elected to put Andy's guitar onto tape next. As an experienced musician, he habitually tuned his instrument before starting to lay down his part. However, about halfway through the performance, Andy, Alex and I all realised that his guitar was out of tune. We asked our engineer to stop the track. Andy checked his tuning. It all seemed fine so we rewound the tape and hit record a second time. We proceeded through the track until about halfway through the song, when the guitar sounded out of tune again. Once more, the tuning was checked and once again appeared to be perfect. Something odd was going on.

Andy was playing to the drums and bass that Roger and John had already recorded, and it was obviously in relation to John's bass that Andy's guitar sounded out of tune. From this we deduced that the problem, whatever it may be, must have occurred after John had recorded his bass. We called in the studio's main technician. He set about checking the multi-track machine but could find nothing amiss. He decided that the problem must lie with Andy's guitar. This seemed absurd to us. We explained that not only had the tuning been checked prior to starting to run the tape but had been checked again once it started to sound dissonant.

We were at loggerheads. The technician was defending the studio equipment, whereas our ears, and simple logic, told a different story. After a heated debate, he finally agreed to listen to what we were hearing rather than looking at what his measuring gauges said. Soon enough, he had to concede that there was a problem, a situation not made any easier by threats that we would leave, along with legal compensation potentially being requested, made by the Berrow brothers who were visiting from the UK.

The engineer went off to make the call to MCI, who made the machines. Although generally considered to be inferior to their German counterparts Ampex or Studer, Air used MCI multi-track tape recorders for the simple reason that they were manufactured in the United States and thus were far easier to keep maintained and serviced than hardware coming from Europe, which turned out to be handy in this case.

MCI agreed to have someone flown out from Miami to assess the situation and run a ruler over the workings of the expensive hardware. That was the end of work for the day as it was going to take several hours for the MCI technician to arrive. Never blokes to miss a jolly, the Berrow brothers made sure they enjoyed their trip to Montserrat, and although in theory they had nothing to do there, I have to say that their clout certainly did come in handy when dealing with these technical gremlins and studio managers reluctant to concede a point.

Once the MCI technician arrived on site, he began a series of complicated tests and measurements, stuff that was way above our heads. He ran specially-made test reels of 2" tape with single sine wave tones of various frequencies through the machine. Once he started these tests the true nature of the problem was finally identified: the tape machine was varying in speed and therefore pitch. There was a complex set of tension arms and wheels that were supposed to maintain the precise speed required. Anyone that has ever had access to a turntable with variable speed will know that the faster you play a record, the higher the pitch becomes. Once the technician had repaired or replaced all the faulty tension arms and tape retainers, we were ready to go. It was a less than perfect start to our time at Montserrat, but we moved forward and started to build up the tracks. Thankfully the sessions proceeded without any major technical issues after that.

As we worked our way through the tracks, I was reminded of the sheer pleasure and satisfaction I gained from working with a band in the role of producer. Having already produced Is There Something I Should Know? and spent time helping demo the songs for the album, I'd established a pretty good relationship with each member of the band. However, the more time I could spend developing those relationships, the better. Part of that understanding comes from being able to develop the same kind of intimacy with them that I would have with my closest friends. Only then was it possible to delve deep into their personalities, understand their talents, overcome any shortcomings and help them perform to their very best ability.

Most popular music is based on a simple 4/4 beat, bars of four beats repeated in blocks of four. A typical verse would consist of either four or eight bars. This structure may vary from song to song but it's surprising how many pop songs adopt an almost identical shape. Differences that were common included making the first verse longer than the second and having the second chorus longer than the first. Some variation could be created by where the middle eight, a different section lasting eight bars, might go. Unlike when playing live, where songs have a definitive ending, most recorded pop songs tend to fade out on the last run of choruses.

Lengths of sections in songs are varied to create dynamics, giving an overall structure that maintains excitement, a shape that is still familiar but keeps listeners interested. The tendency for faded endings was initially developed because of the needs of radio where the DJ would start talking as the song neared its end. As with most things in the creative arts, there are no hard and fast rules and many bands and producers just choose to fade the end of a song because they prefer the way it sounds, rather than just coming to a screeching halt when the track is in full flow. Although when playing live, bands usually build to a crescendo and end with a bang!

Amongst other important jobs a producer does, one of the most important, and for me enjoyable, is to help the musician deliver their very best performance possible. Red light syndrome, well-known in the movie business, is an issue for recording artists, especially vocalists. During the time they are just practicing or running through their parts, they feel little or no pressure and perform effortlessly and flawlessly. But once they know you've hit the record button, they freeze up and all kinds of mistakes and stiffness can start creeping in. In some cases, this has been such a powerful inhibitor that the producer will ask the engineer to remove the bulb from the red record button, in order not to let the musician know when they are being recorded.

Something that fascinated me about Duran Duran was how the hierarchical structure that underpins most groups to a greater or lesser extent, was in their case quite fluid. By that I mean that whenever someone was inspired and came up with good ideas, he could tell the others what to play and they would cheerfully accept direction. Whatever was for the greater good of the track took priority over individual glory. It was fascinating to see how each of the five would take on the role of musical director at different times. Nick Rhodes was more concerned about a feeling or atmosphere and would find ways of describing the effect he wanted from Andy's guitar and let him work out a part himself. Whereas with Andy as musical director, he would often work out actual parts for other members to play. Each session had a character of its own. Many would be a continuous flow of creativity, idea following idea, the track gradually growing and developing its own character.

During the sessions in Montserrat working alongside Alex, I found I needed to adopt slightly different approaches to each of the band members to extract the very best performances from them. Sometimes this involved a certain amount of manipulation. Other times, I really had to get inside the guys' heads in order to help them develop the self-confidence needed to perform to the very best of their ability. As I'd already spent three months working with the band, I certainly knew the guys better than Alex. That said, thanks to his vast experience, he was able to establish his own relationship with each of them a lot quicker than it had taken me. He and I also had plenty of talks alone as we learned about each other. We shared our individual perceptions of what approach worked best with each of the band members in order to get the very best out of them. This was not just in terms of performances, but in inspiring them creatively when new ideas were needed, too.

Sometimes Alex and I would come up with ideas together. In such cases, it was important to understand how best to convey them to each of the band. Andy responded best if you could make him believe he'd come up with the part himself. Roger would just try anything you suggested might work, and then make his own pronouncement regarding its merits. Nick was somewhere in the middle of those two – he needed to feel he'd at least been part of the dialogue that resulted in an idea. As all good bass players should, John looked to Roger as the drummer when new parts were suggested for him to try. With Roger on board, John would try anything. Most complicated of all was Simon. He needed to feel confident he could make the most of any new part. He didn't always respond at once, preferring to play around with it in his own mind first. You could almost see him thinking through the idea before figuring out whether he'd be able to carry it off. If he was confident, all was well and he'd give it a try. If not, he'd dismiss it with some excuse, but this was rare, as by this time he was an accomplished and experienced singer.

Working with Alex in this way, I learned so much about the depth of responsibilities that being a producer involved, as well as the tricks and tactics you could employ to achieve the required result.

At one point during our time in Montserrat, we had a really nasty scare when Nick was taken seriously ill. His condition was so severe that an air ambulance was called in to fly him to Miami and proper medical facilities, since those on the island were understandably somewhat limited. After a few days (and with no expense spared), he thankfully rallied. His condition was diagnosed as Paroxysmal Tachycardia, an abnormally fast heartbeat. I don't believe it was ever fully established what had caused it. We were all incredibly grateful to see him back and soon cavorting about in his normal, happy manner.

Another disruption to proceedings was a prior commitment the management had made for Duran Duran to play a charity concert for Charles and Diana, the Prince and Princess of Wales, in July. It was at Aston Villa football ground, on the outskirts of the band's hometown of Birmingham. This required making a special transatlantic trip back from Montserrat, but one doesn't turn down a Royal command does one? (Nowadays? Perhaps!) It was soon after this charity gig that Princess Diana publicly announced that Duran Duran were her favorite band, a fact which was instantly reported in the press.

While the band were away, doing their duty for England's most popular princess, Alex and I spent the two or three days they were absent tidying up parts we'd recorded, having a bit of a tour around the island, and getting to know each other outside the intense bubble that the seven of us worked within normally. He really was a beautiful man; I could sit and listen to his stories of working with Chris Blackwell's protégés including one of my all-time favorite combinations that Alex himself was responsible for: Miss Grace Jones.

Steve Davey Photography / Alamy

14
WORKING ON ISLAND TIME

While we continued living and working on Montserrat, I loved the time I spent talking with Nick about art. Once he knew I had studied fine art, his intellectual curiosity came out, and we spent many happy hours discussing the various movements of the twentieth century. Rather than a linear history, we just flitted around the various movements that appealed to our sensibilities on any given day. One afternoon might be me describing the birth of Surrealism out of the remains of Dada. On another occasion we might delve into the cultural impact Andy Warhol and Pop Art had on everyday life. Nick also had quite a serious interest in fashion. I gained the impression that there was something about the slightly unreal nature of fashion at the couture level, that meant its exclusive and in large part impractical fancies appealed to Nick.

I think Nick and I were in many ways kindred spirits in our approach to production. Neither of us had a great deal of patience for spending hours editing synths to find the perfect sound. Instead, we preferred to find something close to what we felt the track needed, and then use effects like chorus or delay to make the part work. Or we'd let the sounds dictate the parts and see what worked using these.

Our approach was to look for a sound we liked, some aspect of it would appeal – we would then proceed to edit it or try to layer it with another sound from a different area of the synth's palette. The approach was a more analogue than digital one. I'd be the first to admit that I had not (at that stage in my career) spent much time understanding the editing capabilities or wealth of features incorporated into modern synths. Rather, we were looking for unusual combinations of more natural sounds that could then be combined to create something quite distinctive and original. Some were more effective than others. When I say that modern synths came with a wealth of editing potential that is a huge understatement. You could quite literally start off with a simple Sine wave created by a single oscillator. Then by adding filters and envelopes - along with different wave shapes and many other features - you could (with enough patience and knowledge) create any sound you wanted from a bell to a church organ.

Those early digital synths were real powerhouses however. The early Moog Modular opened the floodgates, and then the NED Synclavier which arrived in 1977, and was the first commercial synthesizer to use purely digital sound generation. In 1979 the Casio VL-1 hit the shops selling for a crazy price of around $70, making electronic music available to all. At the other end of the market, people were experimenting with using computers to control synths, the first and by far the most expensive being the Fairlight CMI. Peter Gabriel was an early adopter along with Trevor Horn, Kate Bush, Thomas Dolby and Alan Tarney. It took hours to program in a piece of music that Alan could have played in ten minutes; the carrot that made someone go through such torture was that once you'd punched the parts in, you could have the machine play them using a multitude of sounds, or change the key, and deploy all manner of sonic tricks.

In 1983 came the ubiquitous Yamaha DX7 which brought in digital FM synthesis after the expensive and unreliable analogue era. Compared to their analogue predecessors, digital synths were far more stable as well as having greater scope for sound editing. The original analogue synths like the Moog were notoriously tricky as they were valve based, so as they heated up they tended to go out of tune. Bands such as Tangerine Dream found playing live with several of these instruments especially challenging as Edgar Froese mentioned many times in interviews. Added to the tuning was the fact that they were very complicated to use, which meant the arrival of machines like the DX7 couldn't come fast enough. Loads of quite small companies started putting out synths and soon the market was full of choice. The digital age was well and truly upon us by 1983 when we were recording on the island, but not everyone approved. Just like the transition from vinyl to CD and from tape to the various types of digital recording, many within the industry felt something had been lost in translation by going headlong into the digital world that involved chopping up sounds (waves moving through air) into bytes (discrete packages able to be understood by computers).

The number of times you sampled the sound per second determined how many bits the waveform was broken into. The analogy is trying to draw a circle with lots of straight lines. If the lines (up, across, up, across) are short enough, the circle will be indistinguishable from one drawn as a single curved line. However, as the length of the lines increases the curve of the circle becomes less and less smooth and you can see each change of direction. The same was true with sound. The early digital machines didn't have the power to sample the sound often enough. The effect was to sound brittle and thin. Additionally, the poor sampling rate would create what were known as artefacts, little glitches that were most likely to occur during the decay of a cymbal or the tail of a vocal's reverb. Inevitably, the digital gear improved by leaps and bounds to the point where people today buy digital software emulations of old analogue synths to recreate that old, unreliable sound (including, at the movement of a virtual slider on the screen, that woozy slightly out of tune feel).

When I describe the technique Nick and I were using as being more analogue, what I mean by that is we were starting off with relatively straightforward pre-set sounds that were attempts at recreating the sounds of real, acoustic instruments like strings, bells, or pianos. Very early synths were an electronic version of a single instrument, like electronic pianos. In the same way, the first electric guitars used electromagnetic pickups to amplify the sound similar to the strings of an acoustic guitar. As the technology was adopted by users, it eventually led to a whole new vocabulary of sounds being made possible, such as using distortion on guitars as a feature, or synthesising sounds that hadn't previously been heard and were truly unique.

The sounds Nick and I were creating often had humble beginnings, but there was a real sense of adventure in selecting certain sounds, then blending them together so well that the original component parts were unrecognisable. This in itself created an air of mystery. When used to play an appropriate part, it often created a sense of juxtaposition and quirkiness that I don't believe you could have created with any amount of editing. It didn't always work, and we often laboured over these hybrids for hours only to scrap them and start afresh. We were always experimenting and learning more about the types of sounds that blended well together and those that needed to be kept apart.

Working with Nick was simply a whole heap of fun. This is not to say any of the guys were miserable in the studio. It's just since all the music I'd created on my own was based around drum machines, synths and electronics, he was closest to me as a musician. We were reliving my New Asia days but on a grand scale. I can't really play at all. It was after reading an interview with Brian Eno where the journalist asked, "What instruments do you play?" and Eno's reply was, "The studio is my instrument," that a light came on in my head. I knew exactly what he meant. The choices the studio gave you, even back in 1979 when I was working at Gallery, were almost limitless.

Just like when we were in France, the daily gathering for dinner at Air was always a high point in the day. In France we were served beautifully prepared meals, cooked by our resident chef. In Montserrat, it was a buffet style affair with a wonderful selection of local fare that was no less delicious. We would all come together and either discuss the day's work or tell stories, of which Alex had plenty. I was always cajoled into revealing more of Bryan Ferry, Phil Manzanera and Roxy's habits. There was a great feeling of camaraderie. One thing that I remember clearly was there being no sense of 'us and them' between the band, Alex and myself. We were all equal on the island and having the time of our lives.

Just to give you a complete picture of what my life was like during our time there, I want to tell you about island life on Montserrat. Anyone who's been to the better-known islands that make up the West Indies – the Bahamas, Jamaica, Barbados, Cuba, Antigua among others – would find Montserrat a bit strange. It certainly didn't cater for tourists in the way the well-known islands did. First, it was a volcanic island – the Soufrière Hills volcano is an active, complex stratovolcano, with many lava domes forming its summit on the island. All the beaches have black sand. This is hardly the thing for sunbathing. If you did any exploring, especially towards the centre of the volcano itself, you were confronted with the sulphurous stench of rotten eggs. Mind you, I've never been sure how people know sulphur smells like rotten eggs because I'm not sure I've ever smelt a bad egg in my life, but there you go. Rotten eggs or not, the island wasn't a place you felt like sunbathing except within the studio grounds which had lawns and a decent-size pool on a veranda. In fact, apart from the odd trip down to one of the coastal towns, the studio, built on top of one of the island's several peaks, provided the best place to spend R&R time, with its great views down across the jungle towards the sea in the distance.

A slightly embarrassing incident occurred on one of our rare days off when I went for a drive in one of the small fleet of vehicles at our disposal. Called Mini Mokes, they were an open recreational vehicle, like a tiny Jeep. The vast majority were built in Australia and even the 10,000 British Mokes were mostly exported, so even though a British design, they are virtually unheard of in their homeland. They had two front seats and a bench across the back, in theory making them four seaters, and (if only because of the lack of any bodywork whatsoever) had a fair lick of speed, as I found out to my cost one day.

The studio manager had a small hatchback, a normal car. The road up to the studio was a narrow, winding affair. I came roaring up the hill on my way back from a trip down to the bay when, as

I rounded a corner, I was faced with the manager in his hatchback going the other way. There was no time to brake and I hit the front of his car with an almighty crash. Thankfully neither of us were going fast enough for it to throw either of us into the windshield.

The Moke had a windscreen that could be folded flat but was in the upright position at the time of the impact. So, had it been a bit more severe, I would almost certainly have been quite badly hurt. Naturally, there was nothing to do but accept responsibility. I was going way too fast for the size of the road and heading into a blind corner. My admission of guilt did little to appease the fuming manager as he surveyed the damage to his car. Thankfully both were still drivable and apart from some insurance form filing, that was the end of that episode. Still, it helped kick start the conversation over dinner!

Back in the studio, recording carried on and we developed an efficient method of working, by combining a mixture of building up the finished songs in the studio and taking the unfinished ones outside, sitting around the pool in the glorious sunshine. Alex and I would take it in turns to work in each of these environments, which meant we both had plenty of fresh air and sun.

It was mainly when based indoors that we spent time working with Simon on recording his vocals. It was an intense experience for sure. There was no doubting his passion, or the fact that he knew he always needed to perform to as high a standard as possible. I was fascinated by the way he approached lyric writing. I didn't have any special access to his thought process, although it seemed like while looking for inspiration he would often just be sitting around in the control room, notepad in hand, writing down ideas and singing lines to himself, much as he had done previously in France.

Once he felt more confident about a part, he would gradually sing it a little louder, so the rest of us could catch glimpses of what he was coming up with. To my mind, his strength lay in his ability to tell stories, which regardless of their meaning, always featured strong imagery, sometimes in a stream of consciousness, akin to the methods used by early Surrealist artists whose goal was to bypass

Air Studios Montserrat Control Room, derelict in its current state © Colin Burn-Murdoch

the intellect and allow their subconscious mind free reign to express their innermost feelings.

As a music fan and listener, I've never been as interested in lyrics as I should be. For me the sound of a singer's voice, its emotional expressiveness, tone and phrasing, words as percussive and rhythmic elements, are often more interesting than the subject matter of the words. Ideally you needed all these qualities to come together to create the overall impact that a great vocal performance can deliver. Singers will play to their strengths by creating a style according to the qualities of their delivery that they value most. Sometimes, Simon would change the style of singing to suit different parts of a song to create an overall effect that he felt made the most of the lyrical and melodic content he'd arrived at. I'm sure

Air Studios Montserrat Pool, derelict in its current state © Colin Burn-Murdoch

every fan has their own personal favourites but one song in which I think Simon really excels himself in terms of adopting different styles for different sections is The Reflex. During the progression from intro to verse, to bridge then chorus, he first sings in his usual style - then come the "Why-y-y-y-y's" like a Tarzan yell that lead into the choruses, where he builds up his singing with doubling and harmonies. It's a great mixture of sounds and styles that make more of an impact than the lyrics, which quite frankly don't seem to mean much and really don't need to. Or New Moon On Monday, where he does a passable imitation of a Ferry-esque croon during the verses only to open out his voice to sing the widescreen chorus. It's a well-crafted song that he really makes his own by his singular approach to the vocal performance.

That's not to say I don't recognise the importance of the words and their meaning. Most good chorus hooks are based around the meaning of the lyrics along with all the other qualities I've mentioned – rhythm, delivery. Ultimately, it's when you have all the planets lined up that the magic happens. When the meaning of the words, their rhythmic phrasing and the melody all combine so that the whole becomes greater than the sum of its parts, then you're probably listening to a hit.

Having spent around eight weeks in paradise, we all agreed to keep an edgy vibe to the album and beware of the dangers of it sounding like the ramblings of a bunch of wealthy young kids detached from their fans. With that in mind, we opted to try and finish the recording and mixing in a city. Because Duran Duran were in the middle of a tax year out of the UK for all but 30 days, we couldn't go back to studios in London. The United States was also out, because of certain union rules I didn't fully understand. So that meant most choices for studios, beyond the West Indies, were in Europe. However, none of us had first-hand experience of any studios in European cities that were suitable.

A plan was hatched. I would fly from Montserrat to Paris via Miami and New York. I would then spend a day visiting as many studios as I could; try and find a suitable facility, then, the same evening, make the long trip back to the island, all within a day. Ambitious? It was insane!

After a long and tiring journey eastward including a night in the air, I arrived in France. I was then driven around Paris to view various studios. Not only did I not see a single facility that convinced me we'd feel at home mixing the album, but the nature of my return flights meant I arrived back at JFK too late for my connection to Miami. Stranded at JFK, I called the Carlyle (of course), booked a room and requested a limo be sent to come and collect me from the airport. I was totally zombified due to the fact I'd twice crossed the Atlantic in under 24 hours. However, once at the hotel I ordered and devoured a superb meal brought to my room, booked a limo back to JFK for the next morning to catch my rescheduled flight to Miami, and settled down to one of the best night's sleeps I can remember. I was living the dream, even if it took its toll over the following days. I had likely failed in my mission to find our next studio, but it was always going to be a long shot. That said, even I find the story of how we finally decided on where to go next a little hard to believe.

A&R staff from EMI would turn up at the studio you were working at in order to try and hear a sneak preview of the forthcoming product. They had legitimate reasons, tasked as they were with guiding the finished product through the corporate system – manufacturing, promotion, marketing, you name it. From our point of view however, these surprise visits were at best inconvenient, at worst downright disruptive, to be avoided at all costs. In fact, EMI even sent one lucky girl all the way to Montserrat to see how things were progressing there. I think she was with us for a week. It must have been a fantastic trip for her, and to be fair, she was delightful, although I think she was a junior marketing person rather than senior A&R.

So, what was the best way to stop personnel from EMI's London office from popping into our sessions? Go so far away that the time and cost involved for them would be prohibitive. It was on that basis, and nothing else, that our decision was made to finish the last bits of recording and then the mixing of the album at EMI's Studios 301 in Sydney, Australia.

All too soon, our time at Montserrat was ending. We had already started to put together a to-do list that we would develop into a full-blown job sheet once we hit Sydney and really took stock of what we had. We worked right up to the day we flew out of Montserrat, feeling it was most productive to figure out the things we knew we needed to accomplish while still on the island. As an example, we still had Michelle, BJ and percussionist Raphael, so it made perfect sense to get their parts down for every track. By now we had every song written except Tiger Tiger. Of those eight tracks they all had their basic drum parts, bass lines, some synth and guitar parts, and perhaps most importantly a guide vocal. Even if they didn't have all the verse lyrics finalised, the choruses were pretty much done so we could put the girls' voices on as many of the tracks as possible, even if there might be some parts that we never used. It was far from ideal and we were feeling the pressure big time. I remember Alan Tarney telling me that the reason producers receive royalties and engineers don't is because producers have to take the responsibility. It's at times like that last day in Montserrat that I would remember his wise and cautionary words from a few years before.

The crew started to pack away all the gear we had brought out to this gorgeous island. After the long flight back to London via Miami and New York, we had the briefest of breaks in London. I took the little time I had available to look up a few old friends and check on the progress being made on an apartment I'd bought. Then almost before I'd recovered from the current dose of jet lag, we were off again, but this time to Australia.

Sydney Harbour Bridge

15
MIXING SEVEN AND THE RAGGED TIGER
EMI STUDIOS 301
SYDNEY, AUSTRALIA
AUTUMN 1983

I arrived at Heathrow ready to board our flight to Sydney. Little did I know that on Alex's insistence, not only the band and their managers but also Alex and I were all to go First Class. On finding out that he and I had only been allocated business class seats, Alex approached EMI or the Berrows and stated quite simply: "How do you expect the band to respect us, take direction from us, or hold us in high esteem if we are resigned to business or, heaven forbid, economy class seats?" They couldn't argue with his simple logic – it was true after all. So, much to my delight and ticket in hand, I approached the first-class check-in for the second time that year. It was some experience, First Class on a 747 meant luxurious Laz-e-boy seats that could be converted into beds. It was not quite the equal of today's individual suites, but by the standards of the day still a huge leap up in comfort, space and levels of service, and included climbing the spiral staircase and into an area with a bar, tables and chairs. Traveling to Sydney was one of the most enjoyable journeys I've ever undertaken, from the VIP departure lounge and pre-flight champagne to the a la carte cuisine with silver service in the air. Mind you, I must admit that Andy and I took some liberties with alternating visits to the bathrooms, to keep various promises previously made! We had an amazing flight that I later found out had cost EMI something in the region of £23,000. In 1983, that was an awful lot of money. There were eight of us flying as I recall. Some bill for a one-way ticket! It certainly was a very special and memorable experience and different to my earlier flight to Sri Lanka because I was with the whole band. The crew obviously knew who they were, and several autographs were asked for and courteously given by the guys which was heartwarming to see.

On landing in Sydney, it soon became clear that although Alex had persuaded EMI to fork out for the very best in air travel for the two of us, they hadn't gone as far as providing us with the kind of individual seafront villas the band members were staying in. I can't remember if Alex managed to swing himself a villa or was resigned to the best hotel in town along with me. It was called the Sebel Townhouse and was sumptuous (even if not quite up to the standards of the Carlyle). I soon felt very comfortable in what was to be my home for the next couple of months. The area was a strange one to choose to build such an upmarket hotel in, as it was right next to Sydney's King's Cross red-light district. Perhaps that is why it had a reputation as the southern hemisphere's pre-eminent rock 'n' roll hotel - and the unofficial home of the Aussie music industry, with a bar whose walls were lined with autographed photos. If Alex did have a villa he deserved it, no hard feelings there whatsoever.

We were booked in at EMI's Studios 301, which none of us knew. Because our reasons for being in Sydney had nothing to do with the studio facilities on offer, we just assumed that being owned by our label, it would be of a high standard and anything lacking we'd be able to rent, buy in or fly in, as required. The studio was as storied as the Sebel Townhouse, having opened in 1926 as Australia's first professional recording studio, with record manufacturing on the premises. The first symphony recorded in Australia took place there in 1950, cementing its role, including the EMI ownership, of an antipodean Abbey Road. It was moved in 1954 to 301 Castlereigh Street, EMI's new head office building in the city. It went stereo in 1958 and multitrack in 1965. An Abbey Road desk was installed in 1972, and like its London counterpart, which had also been simply EMI Studios originally, changed its name to the nickname already bestowed upon it by geography, Studios 301.

Our only real concern was that EMI London had refused our request to have Phil Thornalley flown out to engineer the sessions. This proved to be a classic case of needless penny pinching. I think the most appropriate saying is "Spoiling the ship for a penny's worth of tar." It certainly ended up costing them more, if not financially, but in time and reputation.

When we left Montserrat, in our hearts we all knew we hadn't achieved as much as we could and possibly should have done. It felt as if we'd never really caught up from the lack of songs written in France, or from the technical gremlins we suffered at the very start in Montserrat. The problems with tape speed made us nervous about many parts we were recording and put something of a damper on proceedings. At that time, bands had started taking more and more time recording albums. This was the result of new tech combined with huge budgets for those bands that sold well. The 1980s was the golden decade for album sales with number one albums frequently becoming multi-platinum as a matter of course and regularly topping unit sales of 10 million or more. Industry body RIAA (Recording Industry Association of America) had to invent a new sales award above platinum (a million physical sales), a diamond record, for ten million, in 1999. Just in time for the downloading and streaming revolution that would sadly make such concepts all but irrelevant.

After settling into our respective new homes, we met the following day at Studios 301. The first thing we decided was to create a worksheet with all the songs down the left side, and parts we felt were still required listed across the sheet, showing what needed doing to finish each track. It gave us a clear picture of the scale of the undertaking we collectively faced.

We set out to establish the most productive and efficient working practices that would use our perceived strengths as well as possible. EMI Studios 301 had two main studios and having sole use of the whole facility meant that as there were two producers in the group, we had the option of using both studios at once if required. In practical terms, it meant that as soon as a track was finished either Alex or I could start mixing it, leaving the other to carry on building up the parts to finish the rest of the songs. We could rotate between the two roles to keep things fresh and maintain as much objectivity as possible, no easy feat as we'd already been working on the album every day for several months by that time.

Although not always required to play during every session, most of the band turned up nearly every day and we settled into a period of hard work and high jinks. The 'work hard, play hard' ethos that permeated the 1980s was evident in those sessions, the daily grind often being punctuated by tomfoolery and practical jokes, for the most part harmless, and which acted as an essential release from the constant and mounting pressure we were under.

Everybody was completely focused on the task at hand and the energy was compelling. Ideas were bounced around, decisions made and once a part was suggested it was soon heard and either kept or discarded. Working this way, day by day each track grew and evolved, moving ever closer to completion. Nick, Andy, and perhaps most of all Simon, were in full-on creative mode, whereas Roger and John had mostly completed their parts before we arrived in Sydney. The only major exception being Roger overdubbing some drum fills and accents to his existing patterns already committed to tape, details that created additional colour where required.

The one track that both Roger and John played on along with the rest of the band in Sydney was Tiger Tiger which was created almost entirely at Studios 301. All the guys played their parts, but I do want to mention John's wonderful fretless bass playing which is even more special considering it was the only time he played anything in Sydney. For a musician it can sometimes be hard to start being creative and play again when you have already finished putting down your parts. It was also the track on which Roger worked the most during our time in Sydney, playing over the drum machine I'd programmed to form the basis of the track. Finally, you can't mention an instrumental like Tiger Tiger without talking about Andy Hamilton, a saxophonist who played the main theme of the track in the absence of any lead vocals. Andy had played on Rio and toured with the band extensively as well as playing on other studio tracks.

As each song grew closer to completion, it became clear that we were only going to finish nine that would be strong enough to warrant a place on the album. Making sure we had three singles amongst the songs we were working on had been a priority right from our time in France. Fortunately, the band had come up with the goods and so we had Union Of The Snake, The Reflex and New Moon On Monday in the bag – therefore again we worked on finishing those tracks in Sydney first. Reaching the point where they were ready to mix helped ease the pressure a great deal. It wasn't that the rest of the album was worked on with any less passion or to a lesser standard, it just meant we could deliver a product to EMI that at the very least fulfilled that essential factor of having the singles they required.

So, our stay in Sydney became a race against time, however the creative process is not easy or straightforward requiring as it does the often-fickle element of inspiration. With discipline and hard work - along with the fact that there was the potential of having up to eight creative souls striving to come up with the killer parts needed - we were able to gradually finish adding elements to each track, ready to be mixed.

We were hampered by EMI's refusal to agree to Alex's request that we should use Phil Thornalley as our engineer. Admittedly he was expensive, on top of the costs of flying him in from London and accommodating him, but we needed a top-class technician. The first engineer the studio assigned to us was just plain useless. He didn't have enough experience to come close to creating the type of cutting edge sounds we needed. The second guy was more experienced, a white coat wearing type who unfortunately wasn't particularly interested in contemporary sounds, again ultimately hopeless. We were losing time and patience. The third guy initially seemed like an improvement. His main bad habit was an attitude that was founded on lethargy.

Imagine you're the engineer on the sessions. Music is being recorded onto a 24-track tape recorder and part of your job is to control that machine. So, as we build up the track, we are going to repeatedly want to listen to it. Consequently, after every pass through the song you would be asked, "Play the tape," to listen to what's just gone down, or record a new part.

You've reached the end of the song. What do you think we're going to ask you to do next? The right answer, I think obviously, is to play the tape. You would rewind the tape while we are catching our breath after recording, so when asked to play the tape, all you have to do is hit the play button. This guy however never rewound the tape. Not once. Every time we asked, "Play the tape," he'd say, "OK, I'll just rewind it." We'd have to sit there and wait for the tape to rewind yet again. This may not seem like much, but when the guy keeps doing it after you have already told him numerous times… it can really start to get to you! It's just not professional.

Alex and I hatched a devious plan. We stayed late one evening after everyone had left and set to work. We used to sit behind the engineer on an old chesterfield sofa. We took an empty cardboard box with a lid and pinned it to the ceiling right above where the engineer sat. We then ran a piece of thread across the ceiling which dropped right in front of where we sat. We fixed a release mechanism so when we pulled the thread the lid opened. Once finished we collected the day's garbage and stuffed it into the box. We closed the lid and snuck home like naughty kids. The next day we played the tape, talked for a bit and then said the key words, "Play the tape." As soon as he started to say, "OK I'll rew..." we pulled the thread. He looked up just in time for his face to be covered by day-old garbage. We were doubled up laughing. Unsurprisingly, he uttered a string of expletives and left, which was our intention - job done. It was certainly one of the more memorable episodes of our stay in Sydney, a moment of light relief.

After some debates with EMI in London and the bosses in Sydney, Phil Thornalley was indeed hired, flown in and finally we were able to work without any concerns as to the competence of our engineer. In fact, Phil was not just a consummate professional working to the highest standards, he was also creative. I think you'd agree that after the problems we'd encountered with the previous local engineers forced on us, being able to work with someone of Phil's ability certainly helped the day along and made things so much easier.

Phil was an intense, passionate and incredibly skilled engineer, but he also had taste. He could have been a producer and in fact went on to have a successful career as a singer, producer and songwriter, penning (amongst other smashes) Torn which was a huge hit for Natalie Imbruglia, a Sydney girl by the way. He had the knack that producers need, of being able to hear what sounds are right or cool at any given time. Think of Let's Dance or Is There Something I Should Know? - they both have exquisite sounding snare drums. It's true of every instrument, at any point in the evolution of music, certain sounds are hip. They sound modern, or now, part of the zeitgeist. A great engineer knows this and can create sounds that have the sense of belonging at the cutting edge - and Phil was such an animal.

Each day was a new adventure as we looked for inspiration to complete the songs that would eventually make up the final album. One of the most interesting aspects of this daily challenge was seeing how each of the band members, alongside Alex and I would approach the creative process. In my time off back at the hotel, I would play music on my Sony Walkman, or listen to local pop radio in order to keep abreast of the competition, and as a way of looking for new ideas. Everyone else was consuming as much contemporary music as they could so that when we reconvened for each day's session, we would all come up with suggestions for the parts and sounds needed to keep building momentum and complete the remaining songs.

Sydney was enjoying a renaissance at the time, with claims to becoming a southern hemisphere Hollywood, which might have been a bit of a stretch, but it certainly enjoyed the same bright sunshine and sprawling suburbs as Los Angeles (with a harbour and famous bridge that lent a San Francisco feel as well). Bowie had filmed two music videos for singles off Let's Dance (the title track in a country town 600 kilometres west of Sydney and China Girl in the city); Elton was also spending a lot of time there (including his wedding). The place was springing to life as dowdy 1970s fashion gave in to Australia's love of bright and gaudy colours, as seen in the work of local artist Ken Done.

Nowadays I drink coffee with milk and sugar but back then I preferred it black, and on arriving at Studios 301 the first order of the day was for a steaming hot mug of java to set me up. Mugs in hand, we would continue working on the track we'd focused on the previous night, or if we'd either finished it or ground to a halt, we decided on which track we would tackle next. Our routine was established, the prime objective being to achieve as much as possible in the time we had available. Although on arriving in Australia the three to four months we had at our disposal seemed ample time to complete the album, it wasn't long before days turned into weeks then into months, pressure building throughout. Ideas still came thick and fast from all quarters but the high standards we were aiming for meant most were dismissed and the search for meaningful additions continued. We needed new parts that added substance, not just filler, harder than you'd think even given the wealth of talent and equipment at our disposal.

Everyone had good days and bad days but an aspect of the set up that often came to our rescue was that we had several combinations we could use. Firstly, we could bring to bear the full weight of having eight creative souls all able to work individually. Second, there were two producers and two studios so we could split into two camps. And with eight of us, some of the band could choose to sit out sessions on occasions which helped them retain a fresh perspective on the progress made to date.

During that time in the 1980s it had become commonplace for acts to spend months or even years creating albums and so it was natural that there would be periods of varying levels of productivity.

It's rare to be inspired all the time when you're working on a single project for months. During the lulls, a cloud hung over the sessions, that, combined with unexpected hindrances, ate away the time we had. Consequently, it wasn't long before the pressure we all felt started to become not motivational but instead suffocating; however everyone still knuckled down and worked hard.

Once Phil Thornalley was onboard, he was a major part of the process, able to craft sounds that made it possible to hear the full impact of any given part, blending new sounds into those already committed to tape. Slowly but surely the seeds of songs grew into saplings then fully-grown trees. Like putting flesh on bare bones, building from simple beats and chord progressions into full-blown songs and the album started to take shape. As well as coming up with parts played on their respective instruments, everybody also suggested ideas for others to try. It's difficult to remember exactly what each of us contributed specifically, but listening back to the finished product it becomes easier to recognise the input of the individual band members, and how Alex and I helped them to curate new ideas.

Listening to the album today, I think the aspect that strikes me most is the way I brought a lot of what I learned from working with Roxy Music to the overall vision I shared with the band and Alex; mainly regarding the direction they could go in, what was possible, and just as importantly what I thought sounded cool! How the album sounds today owes a lot to the work I'd been involved in over the previous year or so before starting work with Duran Duran. You can hear it in Is There Something I Should Know? - the low drone synths at the end of each verse bar was a Ferry trick, little things like the sound of breaking glass, just audible under Simon's vocal, or on the tribal drum sound effects underpinning the 'jungle drums' vocal line.

The very first thing you hear in the intro to Union Of The Snake is Nick's almost abstract synth line which could have come straight from an early Roxy Music track. In fact much of The Reflex has elements that I don't think would have been there, like the out-of-tune steel drums or the girls' schoolyard backing vocals, were it not for the influences I brought from my time working with Ferry et al. Possibly the most obvious section that sounds to me so clearly influenced by Roxy Music is the middle eight in Is There Something I Should Know? The sound of Simon's haunting harmonica and the way it sits at the heart of that section wouldn't be out of place on Roxy Music's debut album. I wonder if those of you that know both Avalon and Seven And The Ragged Tiger will find it easier, after reading this book, to hear the influence one had on the other, with this writer as the conduit between the two.

16
SEVEN AND THE RAGGED TIGER SIDE ONE

The next part of the book looks in a bit more detail at how each of the tracks were recorded, and provides an overview of the songs from an insider's perspective.

Track 1 – The Reflex (5:28)

First out of the box: side one, track one is The Reflex, the band's first and only number one hit in the United States. As you know, the shorter version released later as a single in April 1984 was remixed by Nile Rodgers at his cutting-edge best.

When the original album version of The Reflex kicks in, drums and bass start proceedings with Roger and John exchanging abstract fills and licks, punctuated by Nick's synths playing short phrases along with a subtle pulse that combine over the first 16 bars to help the album crackle into life. This creates mood and excitement, building to the start of Simon's vocal with the tantalising line "You've gone too far this time" leaving time hanging over into the first beat of the second line. He then goes up in pitch to almost scream out the second line. All the while Andy's guitar is adding heavy chords and rhythmic phrases. The whole effect is to give the verse a dynamic shape that then leads us into the bridge with its distinctive, warbled "why-y-y don't you use it" opening line. At the end of each three line section is a bar of sax and percussive synths, that after the bridge finally lead us into the chorus with the warning "Buy time, don't lose it", followed by the two bar instrumental section that pans left and right creating a slightly disorientating effect that sets up the chorus.

Like most people, I don't have a clue what The Reflex's lyrics are about and have never really cared personally. It sounds great and is mysterious enough that, like many of Simon's lyrics, the imagery it creates is far more interesting to me than any meaning they may have in a literal sense. Frankly that's more important than any attempts to extract a specific meaning that his words may have. Mind you, I never asked Simon (and don't believe anyone else did at the time) as to whether there was in fact some hidden meaning to the phrases he used in the choruses or not.

What I do know is that Nick plays a haunting string line throughout. By coming in and out of tune it really helps build the sense of a certain strangeness going on. John's bass is brilliant, with his sparse, funky playing interspersed by higher licks at the end of some bars. It sits perfectly with Roger's solid yet flexible drum pattern. The chorus of the album version is a real success. The various parts all weave together to form a huge overall sound that underpins Simon's lead vocal. The girls tra-la-la-la's add a percussive element that, despite being sunk way down in the mix, are still very effective. Lastly, I particularly enjoy how the sax parts during the middle section create a useful percussive counter that works well with the rest of the intentionally confusing nature of the section, as well as adding the new sound and texture created by Andy Hamilton's part.

After that first chorus we have a brief reprieve of the chaotic intro before the track settles down into the second verse, during which Andy adds some great angular rhythm guitar parts to create intensity and dynamics to the section. Simon doubles alternate lines of a verse half the length of the first and leads quickly back into the bridge and second chorus. The most satisfying aspect of the way The Reflex turned out - and a true indication of the solidity of its core structure - has been people's response to the two distinct versions released. I've had a lot of fans say they prefer the album version, in particular the intro. Equally the remix, let's not forget, was a number one hit in both the UK and US.

So, Nile Rodgers obviously added a distinct edge, degree of novelty and ultimately a collection of fresh new sounds that made the track stand out as a single. There's no denying that his remix took many of my favourite parts (like the girl's backing vocals and the percussive steel drum section) and used them in an inventive way that made the most of their potential. A remix can only ever be as good as the source material, however inventive the person at the controls may be. So, it is particularly gratifying that Nile found plenty to work with from the multi-tracks in creating his version. It's a lasting mystery that we'll never know the answer to, but I often wonder how the original version would have fared had it been released as a single instead of the remix? However, it would have needed to be edited as the original version runs to over 5 minutes on the album.

Nile's remix certainly wasn't approved of by everyone at the record label, especially on first hearing. But the band, their managers and others with influence tipped the scales in favour of going with what was undoubtedly a radical sound for its time. It's hard to put it into context now to fully appreciate how shocking the start of the mix was back then. We have become so familiar with the use of samplers to pitch shift and stutter vocals and other sounds that it is hard to appreciate what a shock it was hearing Simon's lead vocal pitched so low at that time. It effectively became more of a sound effect rather than a recognisable vocal part. Nile also took the opportunity to bring unusual elements to the fore and used the sampler as much as he dared. At the time, those early machines were quite simple, certainly compared to the all-singing, all-dancing monsters around today and were still very new. Even given their limited capabilities, people were only just starting to scratch the surface in terms of understanding the full range of options they made available. I don't believe anyone could ever have imagined just how influential samplers and sampling in general would become. They created an entirely new genre of sample-based dance music as well as being a major driver of early hip hop. Hits like Run DMC's Walk This Way, which revived Aerosmith's career, and Paul Hardcastle's anti-war single Nineteen alongside so many others paved the way for a generation of producers making sample-based music.

It's also in the final bridge that you really hear the steel drum part most clearly and the edgy feel that they create with their dubious pitching. Nick Rhodes came up with the sound on his Roland Jupiter-8 keyboard, and whenever I hear that steel drum part it always brings a smile to my face because it's so out of tune. Steel drums always are to some degree, but it was exactly right in terms of rhythm and tone. A wood block sound was mixed in to make it even more percussive and it did the job very successfully! Simon's ad-libs add interest and ramp up the excitement through to the fade.

Track 2 – New Moon On Monday (4:18)

After Nick's sneaky synth note, New Moon On Monday starts with Roger playing a straight-ahead kick snare pattern; a wood block for percussion, and a clever synth line that works in tandem to reinforce the rhythmic quality of the verses. Leading up to the start of Simon's lead vocal is a rising synth sound that morphs into a pulsed line sitting under the lead vocal throughout the verse, and helps to ground the vocal into the rhythm of the track. Andy plays sparse, chopped guitar parts that help add to the groove and reinforce the chord structure. As we move towards the bridge Andy's guitar starts to play a more involved riff that builds into the chorus, which hits with a new pulse from Nick.

Andy's guitar drives the track along and a few tom fills from Roger add to the weight of the section. The first chorus is double length and builds in intensity before the whole track drops down to Nick's pulse again, along with some great percussion work from our old friend Raphael DeJesus, on top of much simplified drums and bass. This brings us into the second verse, which basically follows the same structure as the first but is half the length.

John plays a simple bass line that avoids confusing things by sitting on the kick drum, which is augmented with some slaps and high notes to add just enough of a funk vibe to bring out the danceability inherent in Roger's drumming. In many of Duran Duran's songs, I feel that the chemistry that existed between Roger and John was certainly owing to the whole being even greater than the sum of its parts. They seemed to bring the best out of each other's playing too often for it to be just chance. They had an understanding that is usually to be found at the heart of all great rhythm sections. The pair created a sound that without doubt maximised each other's potential to the full (such as on the fantastic New Religion and Last Chance On The Stairway from Rio). Along the way, they also helped create that instantly recognisable Duran Duran sound that permeates their early albums and reaches its commercial zenith in Seven And The Ragged Tiger. It's an album that on the one hand sticks to a formula they had developed over the first two albums working with Colin Thurston; however at the same time it is full of invention and experimentation that I played some part in, by introducing new ideas and ways of working derived from my time at Gallery. This was further aided by the band themselves, as they were even more involved in the overall production of the end product for this third album.

As the track develops (especially during the first verse) the overall effect is deceptively simple. It builds in such a way as to perfectly set up the transition into the chorus. In addition, through the verses Nick's higher mallet sound combines to create a great counterpoint to Simon's main vocal. This was an example of the two of them working together to bring the best out of each other. The results speak for themselves. John plays in sync with Roger who doesn't do anything particularly challenging for John to stay in time with. We discussed whether the part needed more movement but decided that what the track really needed was a solid grounding. That's certainly what Roger and John created.

Andy uses a relatively sparse guitar part but one that also adds to the rhythmical integrity of the section. I remember spending some time working with Simon on the range of his top line melody, as at times he's hitting some pretty low notes that bring out a seductive quality in his voice that I felt we could have used more. They were particularly effective because of the high parts he sings towards the end of each verse, before hitting the chorus with its torch imagery, underpinned by a low synth part from Nick - and a pulse that sits quite low in the mix but which helps to keep the section moving forward.

Again, as with most of Simon's vocals I have no idea what the real meaning of his lyrics in New Moon On Monday are, and as with all the tracks on the album never entered into any great debate about the subject. In fact the ambiguity gives fans the scope for hours of fun coming up with their own theories as to what he was really saying! I always felt that one of Simon's strengths as a vocalist was his ability to lock onto the underlying beat. He would then either adopt a fluid approach, singing across the groove; or be more disciplined and syncopate his words with the beat, using his phrasing to emphasise the rhythm. He adopted whatever approach he felt suited each section best and the effect he wanted to achieve. Nick plays a string part that creates a chord inversion and ends the chorus with a pulse that leads back into the second verse which, as with The Reflex, is half the length of the first.

It's a relatively short track with a very conventional structure. It moves straight from the second chorus into a middle section. This is interesting because of the way it is in a relatively low key and relies more on superbly crafted sounds and intelligently played parts than loads of effects or trickery. I think it's a real success. Starting out with Nick's string part, again a layered sound that creates an atmosphere that retains a degree of ambiguity, it is quickly joined by percussive parts, wood blocks and shakers along with a pulse. At the same time, we decided to put in parts that were there just to help create a slightly alien environment, the sound that's reminiscent of crashing waves blended with Nick using a Mellotron patch. As anyone who's used the infamous instrument knows, as soon as you introduce it into a song, it creates oodles of atmosphere. It was no different here.

The Mellotron was a very early attempt at creating a synth that used real instruments. The approach was unique. No one had ever tried to do anything remotely similar before it appeared, it's a real one off. Sounds of classical instruments from across the spectrum of a full orchestra were recorded onto quarter inch tape, lengths of which were then loaded onto reels, fed onto a rod that sat inside a gigantic cabinet. Each time you pressed a key, a motor would draw the tape up past a playback head fixed inside the cabinet which reproduced the sound on each length of tape. Blimey, it sounds complicated enough just writing it down and it certainly must have been to make! It never really worked properly, being overly complicated and unreliable, but nonetheless developed a cult following just because the sound was so unique. In the same way that old Moog synths built around valves that were notoriously unreliable were sought after, so the Mellotron had a certain warmth that its unpredictable nature only served to amplify. The tapes would stretch, like cassettes, which meant that even when holding a single note, the sound was full of variation as it was going in and out of tune, sounding a bit like you were underwater!

The machine rarely created a constant note but rather one that wobbled and went in and out of pitch. Naturally, the wobble varied enormously depending on how long you held a single note for, but one thing was never in doubt, the sounds it created really were dripping with atmosphere, a truly analogue beast in a rapidly digitised world. You can hear the effect it has on what is otherwise a pretty straight forward section. Of course, there was more than enough going on to maintain interest and long before it came close to being dull, the third and final chorus hits.

As well as the parts from the previous choruses, Andy added a guitar motif that we all agreed increased the musicality of the end chorus. Along with a collection of synth parts and some inventive layering of his chorus vocals, Simon added more levels of interest by starting phrases at different times during the section through to the end. The result was an interesting outro that both reinforced the hooks of the chorus and most importantly left listeners wanting more. This was always a useful trick and one which had been used before on Is There Something I Should Know?

Track 3 – (I'm Looking For) Cracks In The Pavement (3:39)

Here is one of the more interesting songs on the album in my opinion, (I'm Looking For) Cracks In The Pavement, it's full of fun and a degree of surrealism that really appeals to my sensibilities. The whole mood of the song is created by the combination of Simon's quirky lyrics, like the classic line "Don't want to be in public, my head is full of chopstick – I don't like it!" and the instrumentation the band create. Brilliant! The way the group craft the perfect sound scape for Simon's vocal meanderings is a real joy to listen to, and was a lot of fun to work on.

The sounds and lyrics combined with Simon's top line melody all work in tandem to create a track that has a slightly mad feel about it. This could be the ramblings of a candidate for the local asylum. Bringing back memories of games we all played as school kids, all aspects of Cracks were designed to point out the absurdity of jumping along a pavement avoiding the lines and breaks. Starting with Nick's descending synth line, joined by a low bass note from John and Roger's toms, this combination creates more mystery with the second synth part playing a soft stab, followed by the dissonant line, reminiscent of the circus, which joins the intro and soon settles into an interesting pattern.

Various abstract synth sounds are finally accompanied by Andy's guitar playing a low-keyed riff that helps set up the verse, and the introduction of Simon's lead vocal. As he starts the first line of the verse, there are several parts from Nick including a subtle low pulse joined halfway through the verse by Andy's picked phrase reminiscent of the one used at the heart of Is There Something I Should Know? Ending the verse is Simon spitting out the already mentioned wonderful line above, delivered with a degree of petulance, which leads perfectly into the chorus. Everyone playing creates a fantastic platform for Simon's lyrics. The imagery of memories coming back to haunt him; the second line, "Breaking open doors that I'd sealed up before" sums up the whole song to me.

The entrance into the chorus sees Simon using a slightly mad sounding style of singing that is well suited to the imagery conveyed by his lyrics, another great example of Simon's ability as a storyteller. There's a subtle stab stage left quite low in the mix which along with the other parts in the chorus creates depth without making the song sound cluttered. After a short reprieve of some of the intro parts, the section is enhanced by Roger playing tom fills after the first two vocal lines. Andy comes in from the start of this verse with both the previous riff and some rhythmic parts. He also reprieves the intro riff every four bars to really give the section a lift, building perfectly into the chorus. This whole track is just full of fun and mischief, the jellyfish makes an appearance (you'll know it when you hear it) and it's almost as if the only thing that's trying to retain some sanity is Andy's use of the guitar motif first heard in the intro. Nick brings in a sequence part in the second verse to create dynamics and we soon hit the second chorus. It's one of the most joyous songs on the album and is full of optimism despite its apparently worrying lyrics.

The middle eight has an almost eastern sounding guitar that Simon sings the title lyrics over. The sense of the straitjacket about to be fitted is exemplified by everything about this wonderful song, I love it and although this may be a contentious thing to say to me it sums up all that I like about the album, and some of the ideas I introduced to the band. Their willingness to embrace the idea of something so plainly bonkers is great! They responded to my suggestions with little or no reserve and the result works well and I think is a high point of side one's deep cut tracks. It may appear a bit lightweight on first hearing but the parts the guys came up with lift it well above the ordinary as you listen in more depth.

The middle eight starts with Andy playing a picked part over which Simon sings the title lyric before the guitarist plays his simple but effective solo that seems to try and bring the track back to normality and perfectly sets up the final chorus and outro. Finally, Roger adds some superb tom fills that give weight to the end section before it finally fades. It's about four minutes long but seems shorter which is usually a sign that the dynamics of the song are just right, you never get bored waiting for something to happen.

One of the clever things about this track is that it is deceptively simple, yet all the parts fit together perfectly and show the band at their inventive best - from Nick's almost duck sounding synth in the intro to Andy's guitar solo and the great sound he uses. Finally, it leads perfectly into the next track, which is always a nice quirk to confirm having the right running order in place.

'Cracks' is a lovely gem at the heart of the first side of the album. Although not commercial or substantial enough to be a single it is nonetheless - possibly more than any other song on the album for me - a great example of clever use of dynamics, it builds and falls, giving it a wonderfully addictive shape that keeps your interest from start to end. As I say, brilliant, I love this track to bits!

Track 4 – I Take The Dice (3:15)

Moving on to the next track on the first side, the intro of I Take The Dice was a blend of the interplay between Nick's synth lines. The start also contains one of my favourite lines from Nick, a motif that reappears halfway through the verse. It's an almost clown or circus-like mallet sound that works well with Andy's guitar. That synth is joined by another sound I love which I always called the jellyfish (as mentioned in Cracks above)! We also have a cool percussion part from Raphael DeJesus that is a great accent within the song's structure.

The first verse starts with an emphatic hit as Simon's lead comes in. Singing in a low register his vocal has a degree of menace. It's a track which is a great example of Simon's ability to use his phrasing to really emphasise his vocal's percussive quality. The shape of each line fits with the groove so wonderfully that you're compelled to move with it. Nick's low pad continues and is joined by another synth that plays a counterpoint every bar. The second half of the verse has Simon escaping the restraints of the start, and he lets rip with high held notes after which his phrasing becomes moodier until he sings the title line with a slightly exotic, Eastern bend on the word Dice. Nick's sequenced part is chock full of fun and excitement. It just makes the song sound so positive. Andy's guitar was not a million miles away from the part he'd created for Is There Something I Should Know? having a great shape and drawing the listener in, as any good hooky riff needs to. The whole is bolstered by Andy's ideas and performance on this song.

I Take The Dice is as good a track as any to demonstrate the additional quality a great drummer (compared to programmed drums) adds to a track. It's easy enough to copy a drummer's pattern with careful listening. What's much harder is to emulate the way a drummer uses velocity. In this context velocity is a metric used in describing how hard a drum is hit. This affects not just the volume of the drum but also the characteristics of the sound it produces, its tone. Drummers almost unconsciously use variations in velocity to give shape to fills or in a groove, to place an emphasis or accent on any given beat. To program those subtleties is incredibly hard and time consuming which is why even the most competent programmer will always defer to a real drummer given the chance. At least I know I would! Bang for bucks... a great drummer wins hands down in my experience. It's only when you come across a drummer that's just not good enough that you start looking wistfully at your favourite drum machine over in the corner...

With Roger, he played with a smile, by which I mean his patterns always struck me as if he was really enjoying playing them. Rather than just bringing a good solid beat, Roger seemed to get great satisfaction from coming up with patterns that weren't usually the obvious choice. This generated an extra layer of depth and interest but without making the track sound crowded. I loved working with him and John as a rhythm section. Watching the two of them work on each other's parts was a pleasure in itself. As with any long-standing rhythm section the relationship becomes everything; many people are good drummers or bassists, but until you've found your rhythmic soul mate, you're restricted to playing sessions for existing bands. As the rhythm section you represent the bedrock on which the whole band's sound is built. Without having a pair of musicians with an almost psychic connection, or the musical equivalent of finishing each other's sentences, combined with enough talent to stay in time and tune, the band's going nowhere fast.

It needs to be a deep and sincere relationship where each can second guess what the other person's going to do. When in harmony, inspired and being creative, a good rhythm section becomes a force of nature. When I create tracks of my own I almost always begin with something rhythmic, either using an actual drum pattern I've programmed or maybe a loop of some other type of sound, that still has enough percussiveness in its character that just by being repeated on a constant grid creates a groove. Once you've created a groove the choices of what you do next are only limited by your own imagination. In other words, a groove can be a great starting point for composing a track or song.

Coming back to I Take The Dice, Roger's drums for the intro are deceptively complex. It isn't until we hit the verse and Simon's lead vocal comes in that Roger simplifies things to avoid crowding the track. It also lays the groundwork for making the jump into the chorus where the kick is kept straight ahead with a double on the fours. The part helps drive the chorus through.

The chorus hits hard and is dominated by Simon's vocal lines with notes held at the end of each line. Then there's also Nick's pad and again the slightly circus-like darkness, this time creating images of a ghost train ride! There are several different synth parts that work around each other. I remember that to mix them along with Andy's guitar, and have everything sit well under Simon's lead and backing vocals was not easy. I think it works extremely well and is one of my favourite tracks. The section that follows could almost be a middle 8 but here is used as an effective route back into the verse. I love the handclap sounds which I think were created from a combination of a drum machine's claps, layered with a percussive instrument consisting of two flat slabs of wood that were slapped together. It's so much more interesting than claps alone would have been. Details like that can take a long time and are gone in a flash but done well they create memorable moments.

Before we hit the outro chorus it's the strange but effective middle 8. First you have Nick's low drone sound playing the chord progression, a quick return of that jellyfish and a phrase played by Nick that has an air of church organs and hymns. Alongside this towards the end of the section there are atmospheric sounds that create oodles of character. Finally, Simon vocalises some percussive sounds and Nick and Andy create haunting high tones that all lead into the final chorus and outro. I think it is a good example of the direction the band were trying to head in at the time, appealing to a more adult fan base. This conscious effort to sound increasingly mature is reflected using powerful, stronger sounds combined with slightly more experimental, edgier playing, particularly from Andy on guitar.

In some ways the chorus on this track sounds somewhat formulaic and ends up being a little generic. Although everybody came up with decent parts, both Alex and I agreed that we used the best options to make the track cohesive. It hangs together. But somehow although the intro and verse sections have plenty of merit, the chorus is possibly not quite of the same quality. It happens sometimes, and because we ended up backed into a corner timewise we didn't have the option to start rewriting the songs. The song contains plenty to be happy about. It has some great guitar parts ranging from the sustained note that appears, Eno-like into the choruses and is used sparingly through the track i.e. leading up to the second verse.

There are several parts, like the distorted rhythmic chords, that combine to give the track a depth of interest and a longevity that it would otherwise lack. John plays some funky licks when the space is there, as well as complementing the straight beat Roger predominantly used. I'm not sure what the exact BPM of the track is, but it must be among the fastest on the album. With higher tempos come restrictions on how complex any part can be, especially in relation to the bass and drums. Andy also took control of the middle 8. Using a sustained sound, he played a plucked and picked solo, given extra sparkle by clever use of the guitar's whammy bar to bend some of the notes with vibrato.

Track 5 – Of Crime And Passion (3:50)

Moving on we encounter the strong intro to Of Crime And Passion, with a pumping heartbeat sound fading up into an unexpected climax. Straight away you're hit by Andy's guitar power chords. With the aim of wanting to sound more adult and perhaps slightly tougher, it's parts like Andy's guitar that help achieve that goal. It's interesting to note that with the band's aim of appealing to a more adult fanbase, I think Andy was given more freedom to use a wider range of sounds that he knew his guitar could create. Nick's low synth pad adds weight and leads well into the verse by moving up alongside Andy's sustained guitar note. Roger plays a simple double kick beat with fast hi hats that create a rhythm that really drives the track. I remember we had discussions about whether the intro needed any extra parts. In the end, I think we got the balance just about right. In large part that is due to Andy's driving guitar chords. As the verse starts, Nick's pad continues but Andy's guitar drops out to give more space for Simon's vocals. He starts off with a moody first line, again starting in quite a low register, perfectly reflecting the lyrics before soaring into the second line with the epic sounding shout of "Liar!" that sets the tone for the rest of the verse, which is bookended by Andy's sustained guitar. Overall, the combination of Simon's vocals, Nick's pad and subtle changes to Roger's drum pattern where he starts to drop the odd kick, all combine to create tension. Throughout the song John's bass is working with Roger's drum pattern to again increase the track's energy at the same time as adding interesting melodic colour.

The chorus at first gives the impression of adopting a softer tone but sustains your interest with Nick's sequenced synth, which is joined by a couple of parts from Andy, the sustained line along with solo parts that blend with Nick's synth. We added a big snare effect just as Simon's singing "...afterglow" to create extra drama. The chorus is in two halves, the second part being far more aggressive as you're hit from every direction by often conflicting guitar and synth parts. The overall effect is perfect for the lyrical content -

caught in the crossfire - in sound! This is followed by a variation of the intro. It is somewhat sparser sounding, perfectly leading into the second verse with Andy's sustained guitar riffs.

This verse follows the shape of the first and leads into the second chorus in the same way. From here we have a double length chorus that progresses via a reprise of the intro back into the middle eight which features Andy's wonderfully eccentric and expressive solo. After that we are into a third chorus, the second half of which really lets rip with percussive slaps and additional guitar and synth parts to fade. From the tracks on the album, Of Crime And Passion is certainly one of the tougher rockers, and to my mind is a well-crafted rock / pop song with especially strong dynamics on show. It is a great choice to end side one with energy and style, as the fade drops away into the distance the listener is already keen to hear what is on side two.

"7 & The Ragged Tiger"

"Union Of The Snake"

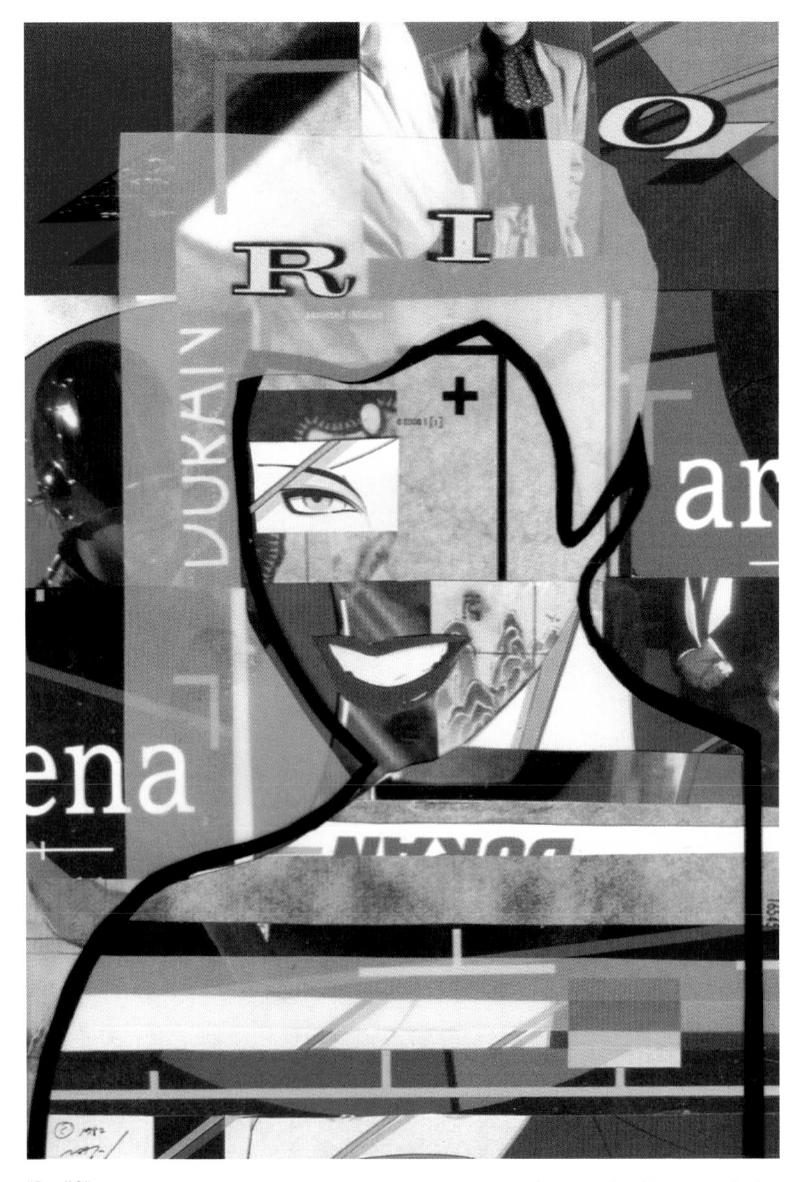

"Rio#2"

17
SEVEN AND THE RAGGED TIGER SIDE TWO

Having reached the last track of side one on the album, this seems like a good time to say something about the running order. This topic is of somewhat less importance in these days of Spotify / Apple Music and streaming in general, although the erosion of the album as a concept really started to happen in the CD age, since a CD doesn't have two sides (act one, act two).

The other factor introduced by CDs (and to my mind, the more damaging) was the 74 minute running time, a stipulation variously attributed to Sony chairman Akio Morita, president Norio Ohga, or conductor Herbert Von Karajan, depending on who's telling the story (the wives of the two Sony guys are credited also) so that the new format could accommodate the longest known recording of Beethoven's Ninth Symphony (Wilhelm Furtwängler's 1951 rendition, 74 minutes on the nose). No band should be releasing 74 minutes of new material at once. There is no way any creative entity can sustain a high level of quality over such a long running time. Many people agree The Beatles didn't pull it off with the White Album, so what chance does a minnow like Justin Timberlake have?

Nowadays people either stream and listen to individual hit songs, or if they do buy a whole album, hear the complete record without that break between sides. Also, with digital playback it is so easy to make up your own playlists. Obviously, that habit started when cassettes arrived and mixtapes were born. But now in the digital age it is so easy that I doubt many people play songs on an album in the order intended as listed on the sleeve.

To finally defeat any efforts the artist or producer may have put into making a compelling running order, you have Spotify creating their own random shuffle of tracks from an album. Unless of course you upgrade to their Premium service, after which you can wrestle back control of the order you want to hear the tracks in and may even decide to hear them as the Producer and artist intended!

The truth is that when vinyl and cassette were the only mediums, a great deal of thought went into deciding the running order of the tracks that made up each side of an album. In simple terms, as with movies and books, each song has a beginning, middle and end. In the days of vinyl, albums were the same. Ideally, you want to start with a strong track to draw listeners in, followed by an interesting track that suggests future delights to come. The rest of the tracks on the first side are put together in such a way that the transition from one to the next just feels right. It may be to do with tempo, musical key or even subject matter. It's not until you are looking for a track to end the side that you go back to considering which of the remaining tracks is the best "page turner." In other words, you're looking for a track with enough impact to compel the listener to turn the record over and start the journey through side two. Ideally, you want the second side to start with a strong track, possibly one earmarked as a single and that generates excitement. After that, the goal is to arrange the last three or four tracks in such a way that they run into each other as smoothly as possible. Finally, you want a strong track to end the album on a high.

With the streaming and downloading of individual songs being so prevalent things have changed. The single has become the dominant form of sales. Album sales have suffered as a consequence. Although still important, I think a different approach to the running order of tracks has evolved to exploit the impact of hit singles much more than the continuity of the album as a whole. As sales of albums continue to decline relative to individual tracks, I feel this trend will continue.

Back to the album and side two starts in a big way with *Union Of The Snake (4:20)* - I've already written a fair amount earlier in the book about the way this track came together, it's one of the most complete songs to have been created during our time in France. Although far from being the only track to have its birth during those three months, it's safe to say it came together far more smoothly than most. Many took much more head scratching and hard work. The surprising thing is that it came about during a low point in proceedings when everybody just seemed stuck for ideas. It happens. It's why it's impossible to say how long it will take to write an album, you can write a song in ten minutes but unless you are very, very lucky chances are it won't be that good. Inspiration doesn't come from a tap you can turn on at will. As you may remember, during quiet spells, sitting on my own in the mobile recording truck I would often keep busy by programming a beat on our Linn Drum machine, both to amuse myself and hopefully give the lads something fresh to inspire them with. On one such occasion I'd worked out the surprisingly complex kick drum pattern to Let's Dance and was keen to play it to the band.

To my delight Roger soon made the beat his own, John joined in with an interesting, hooky bass line that the others soon latched onto. The four instrumentalists worked up various parts and a song quickly took shape. With Simon adding his off the cuff lyrics the track evolved quickly into what became the first single to be lifted from the album and ultimately started side two: Union Of The Snake. As memory serves it was one the quickest songs to be written and Andy and Nick were soon bouncing ideas around, it all progressed very easily, in fact at times it felt almost too easy to the point where I started thinking there must be something wrong. The usual culprit when you have such a feeling is that it's already been written by somebody else! But no, this was straight out of the oven hot and fresh. Listening to the song now, I'm proud of how well it's stood the test of time.

I love the way the track starts with a bang, being very much about the beat. Nick's almost abstract synth line kicks things off and he maintains a simple stab throughout - and a swell at the end of every four bar section - but it's quite a sparse intro. Apart from Roger's strong drum pattern; there's Andy's open rhythm guitar; John's fat bass line with plenty of holes; a cowbell and not much else. The emptiness helps to create a sound that hasn't dated, and still sounds fresh today. As we move into the verse Nick adds a great stabbed synth part that works well with Andy's continued rhythm playing, but the track is still relatively empty. When the bridge arrives, Nick's rhythmic stabs increase in frequency and Andy adds weight with some rocky low chords, both of which help things to step up a gear. Finally Simon drops a distinctive vocal part, extending and bending the last word of each vocal line (a bit like the bridges of The Reflex), before the chorus hits with some great tom fills from Roger; heavy guitars from Andy; and Nick adding a second synth part in a higher register that has a brass-like sound to add edge, along with his original part becoming more frantic. The addition of a cowbell adds to the groove and the way Simon layers his vocals on the last word of each line makes the chorus sound fat.

The second verse builds with the addition of some rising synth parts, and the bridge has Andy Hamilton adding creative sax playing to the arrangement. The middle eight is a triumph, after some feedback from Andy Taylor, great percussion playing and rhythm work, it's the other Andy who takes the lead role with some superb sax, added in Sydney. It has a haunting quality and I'd like to think owes a fair bit to the influence I brought in from Roxy Music. After a short last bridge, the song ends on a gradually building chorus section / outro, with a typical kitchen sink approach, but considering the track as a whole, the dynamics are superb; it starts very open, empty, and ends battering you into submission. It's a great example of how to continually build interest into a song without it ever sounding messy or crowded.

After Union Of The Snake, the remaining tracks on side two are to me a little rushed and possibly the least successful songs on the album. They're not bad by any means, which only goes to show the standard set by the previous tracks on side one. In my opinion, if side two is slightly lacking the punch and variety of side one it reflects the fact that by the time we were putting the last few songs together, time was not on our side - and I know that given more time we could have made those tracks even stronger. It's the consequence of having to make the Christmas deadline. But it is what it is, and I know most of you reading this enjoy the whole album, despite my own misgivings. The album was a hit, spawned three massive singles, and sold many millions globally. It was a major success, but in my very honest opinion it could've been even better artistically if more time had been spent on writing, to at least give us the option of choosing the nine or ten strongest songs from a larger pool. As it was, we were forced to use everything the band came up with, and then make the best album we could at the time.

I think a lot of the responsibility must be assigned to both the Berrow brothers as their managers, and EMI who were constantly making demands of them for marketing purposes and a great deal of their time. That could have been used to write new material on a more relaxed basis, but instead had to be spent promoting themselves and their music away from the studio.

Track 2 – Shadows On Your Side (4:03)

In many ways I think Of Crime And Passion and Shadows On Your Side are similar types of songs. They both show the band maturing and wanting to appeal to a more adult audience. Right from the start with Roger's drum fills and the BPM of over 137/8 this is not a track that's standing around waiting for anyone. I love Andy's picked rhythm guitar parts which, combined with Nick's percussive synth stabs generate excitement from the outset. John plays a pretty funky and complex bass line that sits well with Roger's kick drum to produce a solid rock groove. There's nothing exceptionally different about this song but it all works well as planned and has attitude. Simon's lead vocal comes in with intent, but I must admit the transition that takes us from verse to chorus is not one of my favourites. If we'd had more time, I know full well that the band could have come up with a stronger, more satisfying transition between the verse and chorus but it's still ok and flows well. Andy's guitar adds a degree of menace especially the wolf yowl at the end of the chorus, after which we're led into the second verse by a half-length reprieve of the intro section.

With the addition of an original xylophone mallet sound from Nick the second verse has added depth which gives it a lift over the first. Similarly, the second chorus is a duplicate of the first, apart from an extra synth pad to add some weight. This is a double length chorus that leads seamlessly into the middle eight. On the way, there is the addition of some extra synth parts that combine with Andy's power chords to create a powerful chorus. There's some great percussion from Raphael DeJesus throughout the song that creates interesting accents at various points. Simon adds great harmonies and doubles some verse lyrics too.

After that we have an almost incongruously pleasant, Western movie soundtrack guitar solo that, despite seeming at odds with the mood of the rest of the track, ultimately works well with the parts leading up to it. Simon adds quite subtle backing vocals and Nick contributes with some abstract noises, panning across the sound stage. Although I don't think it's the strongest of tracks on the album it sits in that notoriously hard to fill, second song on side two slot. Having started the second side so strongly with what had been the lead single released in advance of the album, it's almost inevitable that the next track is going to have its work cut out to match the intensity of the hit song preceding it!

After the lengthy middle eight we return for a short reprieve of the intro and third verse, which starts off as an instrumental before Simon's lead vocal comes back in. The song then deviates a little from what would be a normal structure by introducing a brand-new section. Headed up by Simon singing "The shadows are on your side" in a low register (almost spoken rather than sung) there are also some interesting parts from Nick that combine to add a subtle background atmosphere. Finally, towards the end of the outro he adds a high, held string note that gives the fade that extra level of tension.

For all of you that love the song, I have to say our lack of time meant making compromises, and deep down I know it could and should have sounded a lot better. From many bands it would have been a more than adequate album track but Duran Duran were reaching higher standards at the time, and in the context of the rest of the album it just falls short from my point of view. It's still a satisfying track and in many ways my opinions say more about the Producer's curse than the track itself. You always want to tweak a little bit more but at some point have to say that's it! I'm sure most of you love it as it was released and will disagree with my slightly harsh critique, but a Producer's responsibility is always to be 100% honest. I'm not employed to be a "yes" man.

Track 3 – Tiger Tiger (3:20)

Next in the running order is the infamous instrumental Tiger Tiger. The reason I call it infamous is because of the battle that went on between Andy Hamilton, the band and their management about his request for a writing credit along with the royalties this would have generated for him. There have been many arguments (thankfully none that I was party to) about whether Andy Hamilton deserved writing credits for his sax part or not. The ultimate decision was that his contribution didn't warrant a writing credit. My personal feeling is that the band were within their rights in not agreeing to his demands. It's always a tricky line to walk, but ultimately who needs who the most? Without the initial track that the band had created, Andy wouldn't have had a platform to lay his admittedly superb parts over.

The song starts with the kind of abstract, atmospheric intro not dissimilar to a more modern dance or drum 'n' bass track, only shorter. It slowly grows until amongst the high synth lines and John's stereo fretless bass there's a panning synth that's joined by Andy's picked guitar part, with a distinct but quite short delay and just a little feedback. Roger's drum part comes in, playing a pattern, that if my memory serves was based on one that we programmed first on a drum machine. The combination of the sound of the drum machine and Roger's live kit works so seamlessly because the drum machine is very much of that era and firmly sets the track in the 1980s. The gradual build-up of parts creates interest. The track grows until the saxophone comes in, taking the place of a lead vocal and creating a focal point for the listener.

Long-term fans of the band will also associate Tiger Tiger as a key part of the highly atmospheric soundtrack to the 1984 tour documentary Sing Blue Silver, where it is used as a perfect hook for the beautiful aerial footage of the trucks carrying Duran Duran's equipment across the wide open plains in the States.

There's also the different mix of Tiger Tiger that I did for the B-Side of New Moon On Monday when it was released as a single. What I tried to do was make the track sound a little less easy listening and a bit more dance club friendly. It wasn't really the best BPM or tempo to try that with. I'm only partially satisfied with the result unfortunately. As always though, it's the opinions of you, the fans that matter most and I've heard a good deal of praise for both the original album version and my later remix. I think it's a great track to have included at this point on the album, as a song that is quite unexpected perhaps in the running order. The track came together nicely and has a very satisfying solidity and feel to it, along with sitting well in its position as the penultimate track on the album.

Track 4 – The Seventh Stranger (5:23)

This is a wonderful song to end side two and the album as a whole; it is Simon at his best as a storyteller and shows the whole band working together at their most creative. It evolved from a demo written in France but which wasn't finished until our time in Montserrat. The parts which interlock and complement each other so well are evidence of that unique chemistry that existed within the band. The intro of the song is possibly my favourite part, being full of mystery.

It starts with a series of wood block hits bathed in reverb and it seems like a relatively long time before it is joined by the slightly metallic percussion sound that pans from right to left with an echo. Roger's drums appear with a neat fill while Nick plays a pad that fades in. John plays single held notes on the beat to create a moody rhythm section with Roger's double kick pattern. Nick adds a synth that with its slow attack fades in on each chord. As the verse develops it becomes busier with Roger adding tom fills and John playing some thumb slaps. When the chorus arrives, I really love Andy's guitar parts, especially the held feedback sounds. Nick adds a wealth of interest with a sequenced part and other pad sounds, that along with some great percussion work from Raphael DeJesus, create a groove that keeps this mid-tempo track rolling along with a dynamic shape, gradually building and falling again. The way Nick and Andy's parts interlock and bounce off each other adds so much to the finished track.

The second verse grows out of the first with some licks from Andy and great bell sounds with echoes from Nick, then we're into the second chorus which is much like the first but builds with the earlier arrival of the sequenced part and other pads.

Throughout Simon is singing in quite a low register and adds some great harmonies, especially in the chorus and spoken ad libs that seem to create a sense of slight jeopardy. After the second chorus we're thrown into a wonderful middle section. It starts with the track being stripped back much like the intro with Nick playing a plaintive line before Andy's beautifully understated and highly melodic guitar solo. Then we're back into a third chorus which progresses into a wonderful, almost chaotic outro. There's so much going on until the track again breaks down and the last thing heard is Raphael DeJesus playing a bongo. It's a great, epic track to end this nine-song opus.

And there you have it, an album that took almost a year to write, record and mix, working on three continents prior to being flown halfway back round the planet to be mastered and then manufactured in the UK. Albums were delivered by the truck load, not only in the UK, but throughout Europe and the USA, so there were enough copies in record stores from its worldwide release on November 21st, 1983 for everyone to finally buy it in the days leading up to Christmas. As you will know the band's third album more than achieved its aim to follow the masterpiece that was Rio and appeal to a more adult audience. It reached number one in the UK album chart, improving further on Rio's Top 3 position and was the last album to feature the original Fab Five lineup until the excellent Astronaut was released in 2004, more than 20 years later! As was sadly normal for the music press at the time, reviews were mixed about Duran Duran's latest offering back in 1983.

This was in large part due to the core demographic of each music paper. The New Musical Express was into Punk, New Wave and the burgeoning Indie scene; Sounds was more into album-based bands and stuck their noses up at acts they felt had "sold out" by having chart success (as any pop band naturally aimed to do). As such the readership of each paper influenced the reviews they carried and how they were written, the most balanced publication at the time probably being Melody Maker, which, although they didn't always have the best writers took everything far more on merit. They gave Seven And The Ragged Tiger a relatively positive review (more of a back-handed compliment really) saying: "...the album restores danger and menace to a band that was veering dangerously close to the insipid." At the time I felt Rio had been a bit soft because it was very musically produced by Colin Thurston. That's in large part why when I did my audition mix, I made Faith In This Colour sound as tough as I could.

As I close this section, looking closely at the album track by track, its commercial success and the media's response, the most important people of course are you, the fans that rushed out in that December and bought the album. Thank you, I will always be grateful to all of you. Without your support and love of Duran Duran and their music, not only would the album not have been released but this book wouldn't exist either! I hope that once you've finished reading, you'll play Is There Something I Should Know? and Seven And The Ragged Tiger again, and have at least a little more insight into how they were made and what it was like working with the five guys plus the late, great Alex Sadkin.

18
PRODUCTION PRINCIPALS

The core principals at the heart of good music production are best understood by first appreciating the level of detail you need to hear in order to create great sounding recorded music. It's also important to understand the huge difference between playing songs live and recording them in the studio. With live renditions, once they're finished they are gone for good, off into the ether, whereas recorded music is there forever and listened to repeatedly. Therefore, any mistakes made when playing live are usually forgotten, while recorded music needs to be as close to perfection as the musicians can achieve. Producing recorded music can be broken down into four main areas: song writing, sound creation, performance, mixing. Each of these main elements can be further divided into more granular detail.

I set out to be a producer and focused on the responsibilities that role brings with it. At the highest level, when you're recording a top selling band you really need an experienced and knowledgeable engineer. As an example, I can't tell you all the mikes that were used to record Roger's kit, but I can tell you that as producers, both Alex and I knew exactly what sound we wanted and would direct the engineer to achieve it. The more experience I gained, the more I understood about how particular mikes worked and how their positioning affected the sound. As with most parts it is common practice to record drums "dry," that is without any reverb or other effects. This gives you greater control once you start mixing.

Whatever part is being put down, once the sound is right you can move on to the most important aspect of any recording, the quality of the performance. I needed to focus on all the different aspects that make up a great vocal take for example. First, it needs to be in tune as a minimum, or if it isn't then it must be incredibly expressive instead to make it work. It may take a singer time to learn the melody he or she was trying to follow, along with figuring out the phrasing, making sure all the words fall in the right place and never sound rushed.

So you have pitch or tuning, phrasing, expressiveness and finally the overall character or sound of the vocal in the context of the track. As with the drums and most acoustic instruments, I would always record some room ambience, the sound you'd hear if you were standing in the live room while each instrument was being played, from drums to an acoustic guitar. The ambiance would be recorded onto a pair of tracks, and when mixing a certain amount would be added to the sound to create as live a feel as suited the track. Like the drums, I also recorded the vocals without effects apart from some compression, which helped level out any peaks that might induce distortion, or overly quiet passages that could become lost in the mix. In general, the reason for electing to record things dry is that it gives you far more control once you start the mixing process. Mixing a track is the process for turning all the parts into a cohesive whole, and organising the various elements into a high-quality and satisfying end product.

As far as other techniques we employed in recording Seven And The Ragged Tiger, there was nothing especially innovative about our approach. In most instances we used tried and tested methods. Sadly, we just didn't have the time spare to do very much experimentation. Using a top-class engineer enabled Alex and I to focus on individual performances and make sure the band produced their best for the album. I think there is a wealth of talent on show throughout this record. Recording each of the musicians' parts, it sometimes took a few attempts before we had the right one, but I don't remember the process of capturing a great take ever becoming laboured.

While you're tracking - adding new parts to a song - you have what's called a working mix. This is a balance of the parts already recorded, that create a sound focused on where in the mix the new part will fit, and the other parts it most closely relates to. So, you're constantly changing the working mix to make it easier to obtain the best performance and bring out the best in the performer. At times it would require some TLC to boost a performer's confidence and give them the belief that they could get it right.

19
MY FALL FROM GRACE

I want to start this section very bluntly by saying, not as an excuse but more to help me understand what happened, that I don't think I ever fully caught up with things during / after our time in Sydney. I was still very new to the music industry. Less than four years earlier, I was painting renditions of apartment refurbishments for a young firm of architects. Now, here I was co-producing one of the biggest albums of the decade. My rise to this lofty position had been ridiculously fast. I had learned a great deal from incredibly talented people over a short length of time and had plenty of great ideas. What I lacked was experience. I hadn't been there or done it, I hadn't got the t-shirt. I was confident in my ideas, after the success of Is There Something I Should Know? despite needing Alex and Phil's help to mix the track. I knew what sounded cool, I had my finger on the pulse of the developments in modern music, and felt that I had plenty to bring to the party. However, the truth is that there is no substitute for experience and when the pressure really got to me, my lack of experience became my undoing.

We'd arrived in Sydney with a huge amount of work left to do. I'd enjoyed Montserrat, but by the time we reached Sydney, that feeling of being thrown in at the deep end had become more frequent as the pressure we were under to finish on time increased. It's also when I finally had to 'grow up' as a producer. It took the love and concern of Alex Sadkin, who had at least ten years more experience than me, using his wisdom to put me right, but not until he read me the riot act, big time. He was concerned and more than a little angry when he decided he needed to take me to task. In crystal clear terms he told me that I wasn't pulling my weight. He made me aware that I didn't appear to fully understand the nature and level of responsibility a producer has. Our joint responsibility was to be answerable to EMI and the band. If at the end of the day we delivered a poor or weak album, our heads would roll. Not the band's or the managers - Alex's and mine. It was one of the most sobering experiences of my life. I thank Alex so much for acting as he did. Many others in his position could have reacted far more aggressively than he did.

There are very few days that go by when I don't remember conversations Alex and I had about us buying New York loft apartments and Ferrari Dinos. I don't know about the apartment but I do remember seeing a purple Dino parked outside RAK in St John's Wood with a dent in the rear where a motorcyclist had rear ended him when driving into the studio one day.

To me, the saddest thing about Alex's sudden departure in July 1987, aged just 38, was that he had never been able to say no to a new project. He died having recently finished working on yet another new signing (Boom Crash Opera), just prior to producing Ziggy Marley; and never really took time out to enjoy the fruits of his success. Then again, it seemed that being in the studio was what made him feel most alive. In that respect, he came as close to dying doing what he loved as possible. He and his engineer on the project were driving back after a mild night out relaxing at a local club in Nassau, when their open top Jeep rolled at a notoriously dangerous turn in the road that had a cliff face on the outside. The pair were thrown against this rock wall. Alex was kept on life support for about a week but never regained consciousness. The engineer, I believe, survived but I have no idea in what condition. Rest in peace Alex, you were a pure and special soul. I will always have a big place in my heart for you.

Recounting my memories of that time in my life now, even I find it hard to comprehend where my head was at. I know the feeling of being out of my depth was made even more intense because of the urgent deadlines we had to meet. Sadly, as a result of those last few weeks in Sydney when I was certainly guilty of losing the plot on sleeping pills and was on my way to becoming a drug addict, Duran Duran now (more or less) dismiss my role in their careers and the part I played in the single and album I co-produced with them.

My problems really started when, in looking for some release from this intense pressure, I started taking and soon became addicted to sleeping pills. The consequences were terrible, I was either turning up late because I'd been out looking for what were effectively illicit drugs, or even worse, when I did turn up I was falling asleep. As a result, I became unreliable. I needed to break free of addiction as soon as possible. Thankfully, with Alex's help I found a private doctor who was able to give me prescribed drugs so at least I didn't have to trawl the streets. I could get on with work; as a result I was able to help Alex as best I could to finish the album, which we did – just in time for EMI's deadline!

When we were finished putting the album together - all songs mixed, tracks in the final running order to make what we felt was the best album experience for the fans - came the final parting of the ways. I'd been with the band since the end of the previous year, and apart from a couple of weeks between finishing Is There Something I Should Know? and starting writing in France, it had been nonstop since flying to Sri Lanka to meet Simon. Twelve months later, this was now to be the end of my time as part of the world of Duran Duran. Even were I fortunate enough to produce their next album it wouldn't be for at least a year to 18 months while they toured globally throughout 1984. In the end their next studio album, Notorious (as a three piece minus Roger and Andy Taylor), appeared a full three years after Seven And The Ragged Tiger was released - with live album Arena and well-regarded side projects Arcadia and The Power Station happening in 1985.

Despite my succumbing to the pressures that came with the work (and the realisation that I was partially responsible for spending an estimated £500,000 of EMI's and Tritec's money), we parted as friends. We all hugged and I felt a pang of regret not knowing when I would see them again. During the rush towards the finish line there was hardly time for such emotions in reality, as Alex and I raced for our plane to London, where we were due to meet with expert mastering engineer Arun Chakraverty at Master Room in London W1. We were so close to overrunning the final deadline we'd been given, Alex and I were literally driven from EMI Studios 301 to the airport, clutching the two half-inch master tapes in our carry-on luggage!

There are several factors that I think may have influenced the band's negative long-term feelings towards me. By the end of making Seven And The Ragged Tiger, the cracks were starting to appear and Duran Duran would split after finishing the album's hedonistic global tour, so it was not really a terribly happy time in their career that they would probably want to forget. Additionally, I'm still not convinced my attempts to contact the guys actually reached them but may well have been thrown out by their manager at the time – who knows? Cracks were also appearing in yours truly in Sydney as I described, which made me less than reliable from this time on into the mid to late 1980s.

After overseeing the MTV New Year's Eve bash that Duran Duran headlined, I would have nothing to do with the band ever again. My own decline into addiction, combined with the lads splitting into two different bands in 1985 left me to follow my own path. As I've mentioned elsewhere there was an incredible amount of resentment aimed at me when it was first made public that I was to be the new Producer for what was undoubtedly the biggest pop group in the UK at that time. Managers of more established (and frankly more experienced) contenders were not happy on hearing about my appointment. As a result, a lot of mudslinging and worse went on, as each camp tried to pitch their charge ahead of me. This made me determined to break an unknown act, which I tried to do a few times, but the closest I ever came was with Belouis Some's hit single Imagination and debut album Some People.

Several years later, after Andy Taylor had left Duran Duran and The Power Station, he and I were neighbours, having both bought property in The Royal Victoria Patriotic Building. This was a Victorian orphanage that, after falling into the hands of the council - during which time it served as a school - the building had been empty for some twenty years. As the building was Listed, it couldn't be knocked down or externally changed in appearance in any way. A developer bought it, renovated the exterior, gutted the inside and then sold off apartments. I bought one, which I turned into a superb 1-2 bedroom flat with a 25-foot-high living room ceiling. Andy bought five apartments, one of which included a corner tower. It was palatial!

One day we both arrived home at the same time and started to chat. Some days later he called on me and asked if I'd like to go to LA and work with him. Naturally I jumped at the chance, a ticket was bought - the snob in me was somewhat miffed, as my ticket was economy! Things unfortunately went wrong more or less from the start. Firstly, Andy and his wife Tracy had bought a beautiful bungalow in Malibu, I stayed there 2-3 nights and was just settling in when Andy's PA / security guy came to fetch me and I was relocated to a dingy apartment in West Hollywood, which as you can imagine was a bit of a let-down. Then came the first day in the West Hollywood Recorder, Andy's chosen studio away from home. He was working with Steve Jones from the Sex Pistols and on entering the control room, I was hit by this torrent of power chords that I was surprised to notice were emanating from a full-size live PA Stack, the kind you'd see at a medium sized gig!

When Andy and Steve took a "bathroom" break, one of many, I took the chance to quiz the engineer, who after first removing his ear plugs explained all. The pair were taking humongous amounts of marching powder and then insisting the volume was at 11 all the time. They'd blown the control room monitor speakers twice, after which the owner had hired this live PA stack to prevent further damage or mishap! I also found out that the studio owner was apparently heavily into free base cocaine and had a doctor (who'd been struck off allegedly) administering shots of vitamins and other 'life saving' concoctions to try and counteract the debilitating effects of his coke habit. On finding this out I immediately sought out the former doctor for myself, and told him I wanted some heroin. He of course was more than happy to oblige, especially as he charged me $600 for a couple of dime bags! Mexican Mud was the flavour of the times in LA at that point; I believe white Chinese heroin was also around but I only saw that during an earlier visit in 1986.

So, the first day was a disaster - once high, I could just about stand being in the control room. Nothing remotely like "work" took place, it was almost like being in the studio was merely justification for mammoth drug consumption and that was about it. After being told by the doctor that he'd just given me heroin as I had requested, Andy took the moral high ground. Cocaine use was perfectly acceptable in his company but heroin use was not.

Thankfully - and I sincerely mean this - after no more than five or six days I was packing my bags and being driven back to LAX airport for my return flight to London. That was the very last time I ever saw any of the band, despite asking to be given the opportunity to apologise to them for some of my behaviour in Sydney. However, they've never shown any willingness to talk to me and I probably will never see them again. You never know, maybe someone will read this and realise I say nothing but good things about them all. Regardless of how they now think of me there will always be a place in my heart for all of them. I have fond memories of each person in Duran Duran. It is all rather silly and terribly sad looking back more than 35 years further on. We spent an important year in our lives together, and alongside Alex and Phil I was part of this mega successful album globally from a truly classic period in their career.

20
TAKE MY BREATH AWAY **GIORGIO MORODER, SPARKS & LA**

After my time with Duran Duran, the resulting financial income gave me an insight into what it's like to have a six-figure bank balance. So, when I tell you that money doesn't and never will make you happy or content, I am speaking from personal experience. It gives you choices, but after a few months even that novelty disappears. You're left looking at yourself in the mirror asking the same questions you were asking when broke.

As you can imagine producing Duran Duran meant that I earned a considerable amount of money in a very short time. Apart from the year I lived with the band while we worked together, some of which (but not as much as I thought) was at EMI's expense. Just like the band, I lived like a king. However, I was only earning a fraction of the band's royalties. During the first couple of years after the Duran Duran album, I was working on various projects end to end (including Belouis Some and Sparks) and all seemed well with the world.

I can almost remember the day when I snapped. It's strange but retelling the sequence of events probably makes it hard for anyone that hasn't experienced something similar to understand my behaviour. I remember reaching a point when I was in London, on a Friday evening, trying to finalise the running order of the album

I was working on for Belouis Some. The problem was that I was booked on a flight the following day to go to Barbados and work in Eddy Grant's beautiful residential studio. I just wanted to finish the album I was working on but couldn't because of being at most, a day late. Normally this was not a problem, but because the studio (and even flights) were all booked I had to leave the running order for my capable engineer to finish on my behalf. I can remember sitting in business class, flying to the West Indies in January and feeling totally pissed off because I hadn't been able to finish the running order on an album.

As I sat there gazing out of the aeroplane window, I made the decision that when I arrived back home again I was going off grid, which was really easy before the internet; unplug the phone (no mobiles in those days of course) and ignore your door bell, job done. All I wanted to do was get stoned and relax. That would have been just fine and dandy. We all need a break. My problem was that I carried on like that until people started to slowly think that maybe I wasn't coming back. Perhaps I couldn't handle the pressure. I was becoming a full blown, full time drug addict.

One of the last major jobs that I undertook was producing an album for Sparks, Pulling Rabbits Out Of A Hat. They came from Los Angeles which was still their base in 1985 when I travelled to California again. After an entertaining, albeit brief, stay in a motel right on Sunset Strip, I was moved into a luxurious duplex condominium. I also had the use of a convertible Chevy Corvette. Any car nut will appreciate the pleasure I had, cruising the lush boulevards of Los Angeles in a classic American muscle car. I was there at the request of the aforementioned Giorgio Moroder. Moroder is a legend, rightly regarded as the grandfather of disco, the man responsible for such classics as Donna Summer's I Feel Love, Love To Love You Baby, and, amongst many other successes, also penned the theme tune for the hit movie Top Gun, Take My Breath Away, recorded by Berlin.

This was one of the very last projects I completed before my addiction finally defeated me. Unfortunately, the project started off on a bad footing. They'd sent me a cassette with about 20 demos on it. When we met, the ten songs I wanted to record were the ones they liked least. So, who was going to back down first? Giorgio and to a lesser extent the band adopted the view that they'd asked me to produce the album, so I should choose what I felt were the strongest songs. However, wanting a harmonious session and for the sake of some sense of unity, I suggested we choose six songs each and then compiled the album from those twelve songs.

It's a great feather in my cap to be able to say I worked at Giorgio's superb studio in Universal City, and working with the Sparks' brothers Ron and Russel Mael was certainly an eye opener. People born and bred in LA have a character all their own and these two were almost cartoon Angelenos. We set about recording the songs, and progress was smooth if not particularly inspired. Amongst the greatest pleasures I gained from being at Giorgio's studio complex was experiencing his collection of rare and beautiful classic Ferraris. As an already self-confessed petrol head, Giorgio's offers of driving in his stunning, priceless cars was irresistible and I had many an entertaining drive through the streets of Los Angeles, even going miles up the classic Pacific Coast Highway, pure bliss!

It all went well enough but to be honest I felt the finished record was far from being a classic. It wasn't even the best album of 1985, not by a long way. However, everybody seemed happy enough and I flew back to London. Here's the main reason I mentioned this trip to Los Angeles. At some point after I'd arrived home, Top Gun was released and with it the theme tune Take My Breath Away became a huge hit. I was looking through Billboard's Top 100 and there was the tune sitting pretty at number two, and as I read across the credits, saw that it was written by Giorgio Moroder and Tom Whitlock.

Tom Whitlock! Why, I knew who that was, he was Giorgio's specialist Ferrari mechanic, hired to maintain his collection of classics. I jumped up and down with excitement. He was such a nice guy, and by owning half the copyright of one of the biggest songs of the year, he would have earned a small fortune and still be receiving royalties to this day. Tom had bagged himself a very tasty pension plan and I couldn't be happier for him. I wrote to him and he told me the story.

He was in the yard working on one of the cars and kept hearing the famous bass riff from the song coming out from the studio as Giorgio worked on the track, when the words "take my breath away" came into his head. He wrote the rest of the lyrics in about half an hour and with very little expectation took it in to show to Giorgio. To his amazement, the great man liked it and set Tom's lyrics to the music. Even then, Giorgio mentioned nothing about credits or royalties to Tom, and it wasn't until several months later when the first payments arrived and Tom was presented with a six-figure cheque (the first of several) that the whole thing sank in. He'd co-written one of the year's biggest hits! In my letter I congratulated him and reminded him of us standing around and talking about Giorgio's cars, and how he'd often come for a spin with me in one of the Ferraris.

It's a great, heart-warming story and a wonderful example of the best of the music industry - another reason why I feel so strongly that the more young people are introduced to making music, the more dreams can come true.

禄自由自然

21
HOMELESS IN NEW YORK CITY & NEW BEGINNINGS

As I've alluded to elsewhere, I have been homeless and forced to live on the street for months twice in my lifetime, once in New York and once in London. The first time was in New York, at the start of one long winter.

My dreams had been shattered and my heart broken. I had in large part lost any sense of reason. Symptomatic of my state of mind was a determination to stay in The Big Apple. For some unfathomable reason (despite being fully aware that all was lost) I felt that once I left the city it would be the final nail in the coffin. So, I wanted to stay regardless of my circumstances. I figured it was better to remain in New York, regardless of how hopeless it had become, rather than start again back in London.

It's cold, you have no money for food, let alone somewhere to sleep. You're on your own. Except you're not in reality. The first sign of hope that hit me was being offered help from other people facing similar circumstances but with plenty of experience of surviving them. There is a sense of kinship between people in dire straits, because they all know how tough it is and empathise with you. Naturally not every homeless person was enlightened or spiritually rich, many were almost zombie-like and numbed their feelings with alcohol or drugs. My own relapse into drug use, as a reaction to my circumstances, was certainly a major factor in my decline into homelessness.

Imagine my first night homeless in New York. Winter was almost in full swing and I was faced with sleeping on the street. Stop and think about how you'd feel confronted with that reality for a moment. Snow most days, and useless shoes meant after ten minutes my feet were frozen. I had to endure these conditions long enough to collect enough money from people for food and possibly a night in a flop house.

Flop houses are the cheapest form of accommodation you can rent. They take an old warehouse, divide each floor into cubicles the size of a single bed with a foot extra width but no extra length. As only a few spaces around the outside have access to light, the partition walls stop some metres from the ceiling and then a wire mesh is placed on top to stop people climbing from cubicle to cubicle. It's minimal with no concessions to comfort. It's the absolute bare minimum. To make flop houses even more brutal, at 8am you must leave unless you have the cash to pay for another night. They typically cost between $8 to $12 a night.

Before I discovered flop houses, I was sleeping on the street. One day I encountered a guy I'd seen before who told me excitedly that he was moving out of New York and that if I wanted to, I could take over his penthouse! Somewhat baffled, I followed him into Soho (SOuth of HOuston) until we reached a row of former warehouses that had been converted into loft apartments. As these buildings were formerly used for industrial storage, each had a winch protruding from the roof and a raised platform at street level. "There you go!" he said, pointing to the platform at the front of one such building. A penthouse? It was probably about 18 inches above street level. "Lay down some cardboard and sleep on that and you'll feel like a king!" he enthused. I was totally baffled until the first night when, doing as he said, I not only put cardboard on the stoop but also, being a creative sort, built a box that I could climb into. The difference it made to be that 18 inches above people's passing feet made me feel safe, and to be frank, as if I was truly in a penthouse!

My stay in this penthouse lasted a few weeks until one morning at about 8am a loud banging on my now quite sturdy box announced the arrival of two law enforcement officers. They'd come to tell me that the owner of the building (whose front door I was effectively blocking) had returned so I had to move on. They were decent about it, but nonetheless stood there and watched me gather up as much as I could carry and leave. As I walked away still half asleep, I heard a hearty "good luck buddy" from one of the cops. "Sorry, only doing our jobs," and for once that often-misused expression seemed to convey real sincerity.

These kinds of tricks, shared between old hands and noobs like me created a great sense of community, meaning you never felt alone. I was becoming an experienced street dweller. You had to quickly learn the ropes, especially in New York's bitter snowy winter, or you wouldn't survive for long. Finding out about flop houses was the next step up. But on those days (always with the weather at its worst), when you just couldn't raise the rent required, I had to accept nights out in the elements.

I learned a valuable lesson about human nature during that time. When the weather was severe and my needs were at their greatest, I quickly realised that if I went around with an air of desperation, almost pleading with people to help me, they'd give me a wide berth and I'd achieve nothing. On the other hand, going around with a welcoming smile and behaving like all was well with the world, I could collect more cash in an hour than an entire day spent grovelling. I realised that people didn't want to be confronted with the reality of someone's situation if it was so bad. Whereas if I came across as being absolutely fine and happy, they would engage with me and listen sympathetically as I sold them on the idea of helping me out.

During my time on the streets of New York, on four occasions people walked with me to an ATM or bank where they drew out around $600. They would then look up the nearest travel agent in the phone book, go over there and buy me a ticket to London. It's hard even for me to understand the state of mind I was in to get them to do this, but that's how I felt. So, I developed a line that I could use to justify having to ask people for help. Much of what I told people was true or closely based on the truth of my circumstances. I was a successful beggar, always looking as smart as possible and with a smile on my face.

As a result, I took the first three tickets I was given for flights to London, back to the travel agent and basically said cancel the ticket, take $50 and give me the balance. Paid for with cash the agents had no problem in making a quick $50 and pocketing the rest. It meant having a few weeks of hassle-free living, being able to buy what I needed, and pay to stay at my chosen flop house for several unbroken days.

Eventually a young guy, a lawyer, seemed to suss me out and offered to buy me a ticket, but on a credit card so as he explained, if I didn't use it his card would be credited. I couldn't cash it in. He told me that if I wanted to take the flight, I was to meet him on a certain corner at 9am and he'd drive me to the airport. If I didn't turn up, he'd just cancel the ticket. I sat up all night thinking about what to do and decided it was time to go home, back to London and face the next chapter of my life – and that's what I did. I'd lived for nine months through the winter on the streets of New York before I finally realised that I needed to go home.

In the same way as when I was traveling in India many years earlier, I couldn't help but admire the resilience and happiness of people who had next to nothing but whatever they did have, they shared willingly with me. I found myself often being helped by people with so little to their name, but who were still upbeat. The parallels were clear and portrayed a different set of priorities – rather than putting value on a new car or sofa, these materially impoverished individuals had wealth of a different kind. Obviously not all homeless people are enlightened souls, monk-like and at peace. Many are alcoholics or addicts like I was. But there were more than I would have imagined that somehow, possibly based on their faith or beliefs, valued spiritual wealth and leading a godly life as being of far more importance than any material riches. Sadly, as the world has shrunk and capitalism has become the dominant religion, even in India these spiritual values are being eroded as each successive generation is exposed to the materialism of the West.

The only way I was able to maintain any peace and sense of contentment was by staying as much as possible in the moment. Not identifying with my thoughts; the situation I was in; or my prospects;

but instead almost treating it like a test. If the values I had developed due to the direct experiences of truth that I'd been blessed with meant anything, then it was by being able to accept the perfection of the moment and the peace and contentment that gave me - even in this hopeless situation. The trick was to identify with my essence in the here and now and the perfection that awareness created.

One practical way of avoiding identifying with our thoughts is to do something creative. It doesn't matter how good or bad you are at whatever you fancy trying. The value comes from being focused on what is happening around you in the moment. Painting is an obvious choice as it's easy and inexpensive to get started and can be done in almost any situation.

At one point in my New York travails, I met a backpacker who suggested that rather than just asking people for help, I should find a way of giving them something in return. He gave me a battered copy of Shakespeare's Merchant Of Venice and pointed out a speech given by a character called Portia: 'The Quality Of Mercy'. I read the whole play and learned Portia's quote verbatim. I then proceeded to approach people with the simple question; "Would you like to buy a quote from Shakespeare?" The responses I received ranged from outbursts of laughter followed by handfuls of change, total bewilderment, and those that said yes. Not only did performing the quote make me really come to life but I would often generate a larger audience which resulted in bills being handed over as opposed to small change. The act of being creative in this way helped keep me grounded in the moment and all the benefits that created.

Even my short performances of Shakespeare had the effect of reigniting my creative spirit. This then helped in creating the process of looking in enough detail to be able to express my feelings about the world around me, and had the effect of pushing unwanted thoughts into the background. Try it, even though your attention will undoubtedly wander, you will have to keep bringing your attention back to your current reality.

There are plenty of other forms of creativity that will provide you with the same focus. The other major benefit of practicing any of the creative arts is that it's easy to become passionate and intense about them. All of which helps make you feel alive. The same is true of many activities like going for walks or visiting museums and galleries. All these activities demand your attention in the moment and as such help keep you grounded in the here and now.

It's not complicated, but the rewards can be huge, helping you become more outgoing and appreciative of the wonders of the world. In fact, such behaviour can restore that sense of wonder you felt as a child. You and the world around you are amazing.

The difference between us and the rest of the living world is that we are self-aware and have the illusion of free will. I say illusion because when considered objectively the choices we make are predetermined by our preferences. These build up during our formative years and continue to develop throughout our lives, creating and developing our personalities. There is much debate about the role played in the formation of our character by nature, our genetic inheritance and nurture, the circumstances we are born into. We don't choose our genes or the homes in which we grow up. So, in a sense it's hard to make an argument for us really having any free will. Most of our decisions are made mechanically or unconsciously and, in most cases, don't require us to really be present in the moment or aware of the process. We can go through our entire lives on autopilot, and many do.

Consciousness is the arbiter of conflicting motivations in the brain. As we develop, our personalities become ever more complex, like a small business developing into a large corporation. As we learn new skills, like riding a bike, they become hardwired into the brain and run unconsciously. We need this to happen to be able to function. We have many departments, each responsible for different tasks we need to perform. For example, if you feel hungry, the department required to satisfy that desire becomes dominant and motivates us to find and eat food. Only when there's a conflict in these motivations do we have to bring our conscious mind to bear in order to resolve the conflict going on in our unconscious mind.

I would again be homeless when I eventually returned to London from New York, and survived the experience for a second time. Now in my 60s, I wouldn't like to experience it again, but if that became my reality, my now, I would carry on accepting each moment as being perfect. I know the same insights that got me through it then would do so again, or it would kill me, which comes to us all and is something I've never feared.

Don't think for a minute that I'm suggesting you need to become homeless before you'll be happy! The point I am making is that if you spend time seeking happiness believing it can be found in material things, you're chasing a mirage.

Right here, right now, as you read this, there is nothing that could be added that would make this moment any more complete. I'm sure there are many things you'd like. I could do with a new bed, there's nothing wrong in wanting to own nice things. The problems come when you make your happiness reliant on that house, bed, car or whatever. Because in effect what you're doing is making your happiness conditional, reliant on certain things being in place, none of which are currently the case or within your control now. The end result is happiness and contentment are always being pushed into the future, rather than Being your current state.

We're saying well, if I had this new thing then I'd be happy. It doesn't matter what it is, big or small. If your contentment relies on anything that isn't here now, you'll always be vulnerable. Things you already have can be taken away and if you don't have those things you believe will bring contentment, you may be chasing them all your life. The common denominator that runs through my life, highs and lows, is the knowledge and wisdom I was blessed with during my early years that made me realise that the best path in life is one that focuses on maintaining awareness of being present, identifying with my essence or soul, call it what you like. It's that thing keeping your breath rising and falling and making your heart keep pumping. People use many names for this force. Ultimately, it's that invisible thing that distinguishes a corpse from a living person. Something alive has the spark of conciseness that, when you identify with it, helps your self-awareness grow as a natural evolution of becoming more and more aware of being present in the moment.

An old saying states; you can't put a mountain in a matchbox. It's a way of saying our intellect can't comprehend the infinite. Such an apparently meaningless statement wouldn't look out of place in the texts of Zen. Zen is a branch of Buddhism that abandons all attempts at creating a structured belief system in favour of trying to help its practitioners to know truth prior to thought. Direct experience of anything creates an intense certainty of understanding, in your very self, prior to thought.

To create a direct experience of your true nature, Zen masters (teachers of Zen Buddhism) pose mind games for their students. Their goal is to tie the student's brain in a knot in an attempt to create a breakthrough. They use short texts called Koans to create an unanswerable conundrum. One of the more famous goes as follows. "Contemplate the sound of one hand clapping." The student then tries to come up with a meaningful answer to this paradoxical question. How can you understand one hand clapping, let alone contemplate the sound it would make? It's a bit like saying, it's on the tip of my tongue when trying to remember something. We are often told, stop thinking about it and it'll come to you. In other words, stop trying and the sought-after memory will surface unhindered from your subconscious brain. So it is with the Zen student, just at the point where he is at breaking point, ready to give up in despair of ever understanding this absurd riddle - an awakening occurs! An understanding based on direct experience of truth. Prior to thought. (If you have any interest in Zen, read Zen Flesh, Zen Bones, a wonderful collection of Koans annotated by Zen masters.)

So, there you have it, a story of rising from a middle class upbringing, being the first person in my family to attend university, getting into all manner of drugs and becoming a hippy, going on to find my true love was for making music, reaching the pinnacle of having a few global number ones, making more money than some people earn in a lifetime, spending it all in a few years, ending up homeless first in New York then in London, and coming through all of that to end up writing this book and doing so much more. I have never been happier or felt more alive than I do right now.

I am happy in the certainty that each moment is perfect if I accept it as such and that my life has and continues to be, one full of love, peace and contentment. My biggest wish is that having read this book, apart from adding to your favourite band's story from a new perspective, but in addition that you are also inspired to make the best of yourselves and recognise the potential you have to fulfil your dreams, because with passion and hard work you can live a life where getting out of bed each day is full of excitement and promise. Follow your dreams, listen to your heart and take advantage of every opportunity that comes your way. You can have a life full of satisfaction, contentment and that is basically hugely enjoyable good fun, not one full of the typical nine to five drudgery. Whatever you're passionate about, whatever makes you feel alive, should form the basis of your goals. Work hard, be determined, and if you're single minded, passionate and intense, anything is possible. You can do it, you really can!

Duran Duran as you are all well aware went on to have a long career that continues to this day, despite a split to form The Power Station and Arcadia in the mid-1980s, and again after the original Fab Five reunited for Astronaut. The band today is a four piece, Andy having pursued his own path for a second time, including recently becoming a touring member of the band Reef. Duran Duran are still recording new material, and regularly play live although I understand they tend to stick in a large part to playing in the United States which I know some fans in Europe and the UK are not so happy about. Whatever they do in the future I'm incredibly grateful to have had the chance to work with them and am only sad that my drug addiction, coming when it did, prevented me from spending more time working with them on other opportunities. But I have no regrets, there are some apologies I'd like to be able to make in person, but unless the members of the band are prepared to give me the opportunity to do so all I can do is express them here. If they ever read this book, they'll be left in no doubt that I am fully aware of how much I messed up and am naturally incredibly sorry.

I realise they dismiss the role I played on the records I worked on with them in favour of Alex Sadkin and his flawless track record; but I hope they can remember the good times we had together in London, France and Montserrat, before I went off the rails towards the end of our time in Sydney.

I wish them continued health, wealth and happiness. I'd relish the chance to work with them again; it's not about the money but I still feel, having just heard Invisible their latest single release, that I understand how the chemistry between them works. I have a very dear friend Matt Thompson who writes for K Pop bands including BTS, and in many ways BTS are the closest thing around now to what Duran Duran were about in 1982-1984. I'd happily remix a track, as I did in the first instance, but I realise that's highly unlikely!

When all's said and done I had an amazing time, and it was undoubtedly one of the most intense, insightful years in my life. There's no point talking about 'what if' - you can't change the past or undo bad decisions so I see no point in beating myself up about mine. All I know is that as a result of what they saw in me after hearing my mix of Faith In This Colour, Duran Duran gave me a once in a lifetime opportunity to work on a smash hit single and a multi-platinum album that went to the top spot around the world. Not too many people can say that, I know how blessed I've been. I can't wait to hear Future Past, due for release in October 2021. Great move to work with the legend that is "my friends call me...Giorgio" on some of the new tracks, alongside Mark Ronson again and Erol Alkan to keep things bang up to date!

Thank you so much for buying and reading my book, I hope you have gained some pleasure from, and more importantly fresh insights into both Duran Duran at that pivotal point in their career and the making of two of their most important records. I also hope that I've made you aware how important it is to follow your heart, be at one with your True Self, content and at peace with the world around you.

Finally, remember to laugh (A LOT!) - love and live life to the full. Peace & Love, Ian

ACKNOWLEDGEMENTS

Saying thank you is a fundamental to this book - when fundamental is used to describe something without which the entirety would cease to exist.

Firstly, a Special Commendation must be made to my publisher Charles Kennedy, proprietor of Astral Horizon Press, for his editing, encouragement, knowledge and unquestioning support.

Another Special Commendation for Steve Thorpe for his perspective, knowledge, editing skills and constant encouragement.

A Commendation is justifiably awarded to Murray Wellwood for finding the strength to put product ahead of personal benefit, and creating the stunning cover design for this book.

Sharing the role of creating the physical presence is Simon De Rudder, who has done a fantastic job of designing the inside of this book.

Thanks to Bhavna Vadher, Mathew Butler and Steve Finnigan at Astral Horizon Press for their work behind the scenes to keep the wheels turning.

Huge thanks to Jonas Nilsson (J. Flock) for his stunning Duran Duran artwork on pages 190-192, and the painting which influenced the design of the deluxe edition slipcase. Contact Jonas and buy copies of his prints at www.jflock.se

Too many people influenced the course of my life and combined to reveal paths, point out signposts and create opportunities to list them all. In no particular order (and with many omissions I'm sure) here is my thank you list.

Rosamond Gladys Stonestreet-Little adopted me as a six month old baby, with her husband Harry, and a more enlightened couple I could not imagine bringing me into their home. Not only did I never want for love or affection, they allowed me the freedom to flourish. Harry Little, my dad, died when I was 11 but gave me a vision of speed, edginess and adventure. He was a Royal Navy man. The only other meaningful ties I have now are with my nephews, Rob Francis and Tony Little – my family.

Robin Gray, Paul Davies, and Allan Baine for having faith in me. Phil Manzanera for kick-starting my career in the recording industry; this book wouldn't exist if you hadn't taken a huge chance on me! Andy Mackay for revealing the dark arts of classical music. Bryan Ferry for showing me how to curate performances from some of the best musicians I ever saw play, legends of their times, including Neil Hubbard, Alan Spenner and Andy Newmark. I also want to thank Bryan for recognising my contribution during the creation of Avalon, and the ability to keep a secret! Rhett Davies, using his years of experience to teach a total beginner as much about producing and engineering as he possibly could.

Alan Tarney for teaching me how to write great songs versus adequate songs, and how to tell the difference between them! Plus, more than anyone else I had the pleasure of working with, for teaching me about the art of songwriting. Kevin Godley and Lol Creme for showing me you could have fun and still be creative. Peter Kent for signing me as New Asia to Situation 2, who I also thank for sending me to New York to promote the album and to do interviews on college radio. Various musicians I've met over the last 40 years, thanks for letting me record you and get such great performances from each and every one of you. Magical. Matty Thompson for being an inspiration.

Nick, John, Simon, Roger and Andy, collectively known as Duran Duran, who I had the privilege to know as individuals during possibly the stand-out year of their lives.

Alex Sadkin for having heart and empathy in a world full of narcissism. Phil Thornally for having a great set of ears, and especially helping me to understand how a good mix comes together. Bob

Clearmountain for sharing some of his mixing tricks at the peak of his powers. RAK engineer Pete Schwier. Dave Ambrose and all at EMI. Steve Sutherland and Richard Buskin (journalists), Tony Mottram and Martyn Goddard (photographers). John Robinson of Clique Productions, a dear friend and the best engineer I know today. John Pepper aka DJ Jon, another good friend, Duran Duran fan and creative soul. A very special thanks to Giorgio Moroder for his positive words about this book, I feel honoured to have an endorsement from such a living legend of the music business. Dan from Track By Track Podcasts for inviting me to be involved in Duran Duran's eponymous debut celebration. James Bott's Honest Creative. Christina Wiggins and David Baird for their work on my early ramblings. And finally Giorgio Mercanti and other super fans who told me to carry on after certain parties wanted me to stop.

Friend and professional researcher Lisa Savage for using her immensely persuasive ways to help us find some special images, whilst being a supporter throughout. She and I know how important it was she didn't forget us! And Malcolm Garrett and Keith Breeden for their kind permission for the use of symbols from the original Duran Duran designs.

There are likely many people I've forgotten and I'm sorry, but all I can say is I remember everyone that's ever helped me at one point or another so you're still in my thoughts!

Thanks again all of you. Peace & Love, Ian

MUSIC OUTREACH PROJECT
A BRIEF SYNOPSIS

A few years ago, I had an idea of how it could be possible to engage the disenfranchised young people at the heart of London's growing gang culture. It is my belief that most people joining gangs do so because of peer pressure, combined with a perceived and often real lack of opportunity.

There are many individuals who, whilst lacking academic ability, have a creative spirit that has largely remained dormant through their formative years and into adulthood - simply because they've never been actively encouraged; had mentors; or found ways to express their artistic ideas or develop any real passion for their interest in the arts.

Those most vulnerable to being drawn into gangs, the target group, however are passionate about music – it's part of their culture and everyday lives.

One of the main motivations for writing Baptism Of Fire has been to raise awareness of, and funding for, the Music Outreach Project which is very close to my heart. By revealing the process of employing a computer-based DAW (Digital Audio Workstation) that record producers, bands and songwriters use to create their songs, I can demonstrate that making music is something within these young people's reach.

I aim to show them that learning how to create music using a DAW means that they too could follow the path many of their musical heroes took to achieve success – people like Stormzy or Tiny Tempah. Not everyone will become a star of course, but there are plenty of working musicians who, by using the internet to sell directly to their fans, are able to earn a reasonable living from their music. Many young people lack direction or purpose in their lives and these are the ones who would benefit most from the project. They are also the group most likely to end up in gangs if they can't find a way to engage with something they can become passionate about and that could, with effort, lead to meaningful work. The fact they are already into music gives this project the potential to become a powerful part of a wider solution to this ever-growing problem of law breaking and senseless killings.

My idea is to create a portable DAW that I could set up in any community space and run sessions, free to end users and lasting anything between a day or several weeks. Class sizes of 6-10 individuals would be ideal as it would enable every attendee to get involved. The key to the system I have specified is that it contains plenty of scope for interactivity, so all involved can feel proud of the end product and cultivate a shared sense of ownership. A video could also be made, both as a record of the lessons and to accompany any worthwhile pieces of music created. These videos would act as "calling cards" demonstrating the process in action and showing its efficacy to others facing similar problems.

The lessons would be designed to demonstrate that with relatively little equipment and a minimal amount of training they too could express their artistic nature by creating music. This would not only open up pathways into the music industry, but the many other creative businesses such as film making, graphics, fashion design, and the huge variety of creative arts for which London is a recognised global leader, employing thousands of people and generating wealth for the country.

Offering young people the opportunity to express themselves artistically would give them a much needed sense of self-worth and help them realise that they do have choices, can take control of their lives, and create opportunities that could eventually lead to meaningful work. Thank you for buying this book, and helping to make the Music Outreach Project become a reality soon.

DURAN DURAN DISCOGRAPHY 1981 TO 1985
COMPILED BY STEVE THORPE

SINGLES **1981**

PLANET EARTH / LATE BAR (EMI 5137) Released February 2

Entered UK Top 40 week end March 14 #26 (#1 Roxy Music Jealous Guy*)

Peak #12 week ending March 28 (#1 Shakin' Stevens This Ole House)

11 weeks on chart

CARELESS MEMORIES / KHANADA (EMI 5168) Released April 20

Entered UK Top 40 week ending May 16 #38 (#1 Adam & the Ants – Stand And Deliver)

Peak #37 week ending May 23 (#1 Adam & the Ants remain)

7 weeks on chart

GIRLS ON FILM / FASTER THAN LIGHT (EMI 5206) Released July 13

Entered UK Top 40 week ending July 25 #29 (#1 Specials – Ghost Town)

Peak #5 week ending August 22 (#1 Shakin' Stevens – Green Door)

11 weeks on chart

MY OWN WAY / LIKE AN ANGEL (EMI 5254) Released November 16

Entered UK Top 40 week ending November 28 #37 (#1 Queen + David Bowie – Under Pressure)

Peak #14 week ending December 19 (#1 Human League – Don't You Want Me)

11 weeks on chart

SINGLES **1982**

HUNGRY LIKE THE WOLF / CARELESS MEMORIES (LIVE) (EMI 5295) Released May 4

Entered UK Top 40 week ending May 15 #35 (#1 Nicole – A Little Peace)

Peak #5 week ending June 26 (#1 Charlene – I've Never Been To Me)

12 weeks on chart

SAVE A PRAYER / HOLD BACK THE RAIN (REMIX) (EMI 5327) Released August 9

Entered UK Top 40 week ending August 21 #27 (#1 Dexy's Midnight Runners – Come On Eileen)

Peak #2 week ending September 11 (#1 Survivor – Eye of the Tiger)

9 weeks on chart

RIO / THE CHAUFFEUR (BLUE SILVER) (EMI 5346)
Released November 1

Entered UK Top 40 week ending November 13 #32 (#1 Eddy Grant – I Don't Wanna Dance)

Peak #9 week ending December 11 (#1 The Jam – Beat Surrender)

11 weeks on chart

SINGLES **1983**

IS THERE SOMETHING I SHOULD KNOW? /
FAITH IN THIS COLOUR (EMI 5371)* Released March 19

Entered UK Top 40 week ending March 16 Peak #1 during a 9 week run

#2: Total Eclipse of the Heart, Bonnie Tyler; #3 Sweet Dreams (Are Made Of This), Eurythmics; #4 Speak Like A Child, Style Council; #5 Let's Dance, David Bowie

UNION OF THE SNAKE / SECRET OKTOBER (EMI 5429)* Released October 17

Entered UK Top 40 week ending October 29 #4 (#1 Culture Club – Karma Chameleon)

Peak #3 week ending November 5 (#1 Billy Joel – Uptown Girl)

11 weeks on chart

SINGLES **1984**

NEW MOON ON MONDAY / TIGER TIGER (IAN LITTLE REMIX) (EMI DURAN 1)* Released January 23

Entered UK Top 40 week ending February 4 #12 (#1 Frankie Goes To Hollywood – Relax)

Peak #9 week ending February 11 (#1 Frankie Goes To Hollywood)

7 weeks on chart

THE REFLEX (REMIX) / MAKE ME SMILE (COME UP AND SEE ME) (LIVE) (EMI DURAN 2)* Released April 16

Entered UK Top 40 week ending April 28 #5 (#1 Lionel Richie – Hello)

Peak #1 week ending May 5 during a 14 week run

2 Against All Odds (Take A Look At Me Now), Phil Collins; #3: I Want To Break Free, Queen; #4: Hello, Lionel Richie; #5: Automatic, Pointer Sisters

THE WILD BOYS / (I'M LOOKING FOR) CRACKS IN THE PAVEMENT (PARLOPHONE DURAN 3) Released October 26

Entered UK Top 40 week ending November 3 #5 (#1 Wham! – Freedom)

Peak #2 week ending November 17 (#1 Chaka Khan – I Feel For You)

14 weeks on chart

SINGLES **1985**

A VIEW TO A KILL / THAT FATAL KISS (PARLOPHONE DURAN 007) Released May 6

Entered UK Top 40 week ending May 18 #7 (#1 Paul Hardcastle – 19)

Peak #2 week ending May 25 (#1 Paul Hardcastle remains)

16 weeks on chart

ALBUMS **1981-1984**

DURAN DURAN (EMI - EMC 3372) Released June 15, 1981

GIRLS ON FILM / PLANET EARTH / ANYONE OUT THERE / TO THE SHORE / CARELESS MEMORIES / NIGHTBOAT / SOUND OF THUNDER / FRIENDS OF MINE / TEL AVIV

Peak #3, 118 weeks on chart

RIO (EMI - EMC 3411) Released May 10, 1982

RIO / MY OWN WAY / LONELY IN YOUR NIGHTMARE / HUNGRY LIKE THE WOLF / HOLD BACK THE RAIN / NEW RELIGION / LAST CHANCE ON THE STAIRWAY / SAVE A PRAYER / THE CHAUFFEUR

Peak #2, 109 weeks on chart

SEVEN AND THE RAGGED TIGER (EMI DD 1)* Released November 21, 1983

THE REFLEX / NEW MOON ON MONDAY / (I'M LOOKING FOR) CRACKS IN THE PAVEMENT / I TAKE THE DICE / OF CRIME AND PASSION / UNION OF THE SNAKE / SHADOWS ON YOUR SIDE / TIGER TIGER / THE SEVENTH STRANGER

Peak #1, 47 weeks on chart

ARENA (PARLOPHONE DD 2) Released November 12, 1984

IS THERE SOMETHING I SHOULD KNOW? / HUNGRY LIKE THE WOLF / NEW RELIGION / SAVE A PRAYER / THE WILD BOYS / THE SEVENTH STRANGER / THE CHAUFFEUR / UNION OF THE SNAKE / PLANET EARTH / CARELESS MEMORIES

Peak #6, 31 weeks on chart

All live recordings except for The Wild Boys

* Ian Little production credit